Sir Algernon Methuen

# A
# *Thousand*
# *Capricious*
# *Chances*

A History of the Methuen List

1889–1989

MAUREEN DUFFY

Methuen London

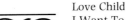

*by*
*the same*
*author*

That's How it Was
The Single Eye
The Microcosm
The Paradox Players
Love Child
I Want To Go To Moscow
Capital
Housespy
Lyrics for the Dog Hour
The Venus Touch
The Erotic World of Faery
Evensong
The Passionate Shepherdess
Memorials of the Quick and the Dead
Inherit the Earth
Rites
Solo
A Nightingale in Bloomsbury Square
Gor Saga
Londoners
Change
Men and Beasts: Collected Poems 1949–84

First published in Great Britain 1989
by Methuen London Ltd
Michelin House, 81 Fulham Road, London SW3 6RB
Copyright © 1989 Maureen Duffy

Printed in Great Britain
by Butler & Tanner Ltd, Frome

Designed by Christopher Holgate

A CIP catalogue record for this book
is available from the British Library

ISBN 0 413 573508

# Contents

# Illustrations

The publishers would like to thank those who have helped with the location of archive material, particularly Mrs M. Miller for the illustrations reproduced on pages x, 20, 26, 51, 59, 82; the estate of C. W. Chamberlain for the illustrations reproduced on pages 50, 56, 69, 79, 125; and Frank Herrmann for the illustrations reproduced on page 145. In the case of copyright material – both illustrative and textual – every effort has been made to trace copyright holders. Apologies are made for any errors or omissions. Where books have been illustrated, the date given in brackets is that of the edition reproduced. In some cases this is the first edition; in others, a later edition.

'Why is it that every other profession can be taken seriously,
but that a novelist's work is supposed to be mere play?
Good God! don't we suffer enough?
Have we not hard brain work and drudgery of desk work
and tedious gathering of statistics
and troublesome search into details?
Have we not an appalling weight of responsibility upon us?
– and are we not at the mercy of a thousand capricious chances?'
*Derrick Vaughan, Novelist*
Edna Lyall

# *Preface*

The history of any cultural institution is a combination of internal and external elements, of the people who run it and the outside pressures they must respond to. It exists not for itself but to present creative work to the public, whether music, dance, drama, painting and sculpture or, as in the case of a publishing house, literary works of imagination and information. Unlike other commercial enterprises whose primary purpose is to make money for their proprietors, either individual or collective, the organisation for creating or purveying culture can exist virtually without financial profit as long as it continues to fulfil its initial function, and indeed it is almost in the nature of such institutions that much of the time their commercial profitability may be in doubt. It is the product itself which is the profit. Seen from this point of view, what is important in the history of a cultural institution is what it has enabled its artists to achieve and present, and it is for this that it will be remembered.

The history of Methuen I see, therefore, as embodied in the authors and titles which it has published over the last century, and a close study of them shows the external and internal factors at work. Books are expressions not just of the individual but of the collective consciousness as well, and they reflect both the personal concerns of the author and those of the society in which the work appears at a precise historical, social and cultural time and place. A study of the list of one general publishing house gives us the story of our times filtered through the personalities of those who have run the company, and principally, of course, those who have made the editorial choices and the authors they have chosen.

I have tried not simply to write a company history but rather to set Methuen and its list in its historical context, and I must now thank those, both the living and the dead, who have helped me in this. First must come Geoffrey Strachan, the present publisher, whose ambition it has been for several years to have a history of the company and who initiated the series of historical interviews by Anthony Seldon with past employees which I have found invaluable. Next I must thank Michael Turner, J. Alan White and Peter Wait, who allowed me to interview them and delve into their memories. I was also able to draw on the written memorials of E. J. Taylor, Halfdan Lynner, Tony Forster, Peter Wait again, and J. Alan White's invaluable brief history, given as part of a management training course in 1964.

I must also thank David Sampson, the company secretary of Associated Book Publishers until his retirement in 1988, and in particular Sheila Knatt, who had charge until recently of the archives and file room at the company warehouse in Andover, and who was unfailingly cheerful and helpful during my constant raids on her carefully maintained records.

Finally I should like to thank the estate of C. W. Chamberlain and Mrs M. Miller for the use of their privately owned illustrative material.

London 1989

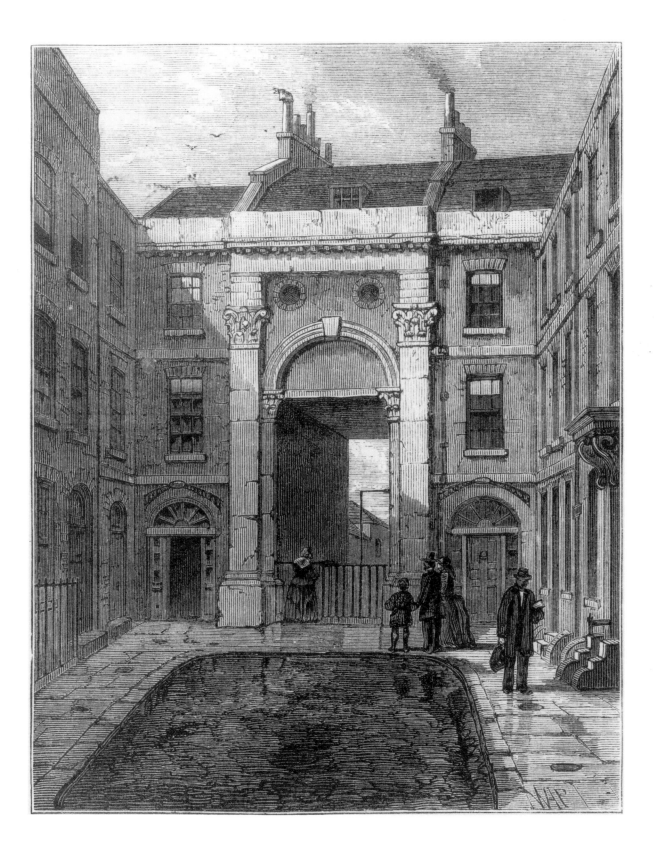

# ONE

# The First Decade
## 1889–99

Buried not too deep in the collective unconscious of authors, as it was once correct to call them, writers as they have more recently and democratically become, is an aboriginal dreamtime, a Golden Age, if not a Garden of Eden, in which horticulture must have left little time for reading and writing, when there were only writers and readers with no publisher to come between. The pull of this myth is so strong that it sometimes paradoxically causes writers to become publishers. The founding of Methuen and Company in June 1889 was just such a manifestation.

Algernon Methuen Marshall Stedman was born a third son on 23 February 1856 at 171 Union Street, Southwark. The Methuen part was a family name handed down from the daughter Mary of John Methuen who had negotiated a treaty named after him with Portugal in 1709. Algernon's father, John Buck Stedman, was a doctor and at one time mayor of Godalming. His mother was Jane Elizabeth, daughter of Richard Marshall of King's Lynn. Young Algernon was obviously a bookish child and produced his first oeuvre, a Greek grammar, at the age of eight. He went to Berkhamsted School in 1869 and then on to Wadham College, Oxford when he was seventeen where, not surprisingly, he took, in 1878, a degree in Classics. His first job, as a tutor in a coaching establishment, Friar Park in Henley-on-Thames, apparently left him time to take up his career as a writer again and he produced a book on Oxford which was published by Trübner and Co. in 1878. It was described as one of 'considerable audacity which was received with severe criticism'. Stedman himself, anticipating this in his preface, wrote: 'The chapters on Oxford life will probably not meet with universal approval. The author has only to plead the extreme difficulty and delicacy of the subject; for himself, he has attempted to steer between a severe Puritanism and a vulgar flippancy, and to judge impartially between good points and bad.'

In 1880 he started his own prep school, Highcroft, at Milford near Godalming, and began to write (often it seems during lesson time while the boys were given something to get on with) his own textbooks, which he had printed at his own

expense and distributed from the school until he handed this operation over to George Bell and Sons, though whether at their suggestion or his doesn't seem to have been recorded. However, school textbook production didn't sufficiently satisfy his literary ambitions and he decided to re-edit his book on Oxford.

While doing this, and in particular taken with the chapter contributed on the history of the university by Herbert Hensley Henson, Fellow of All Souls and future Bishop of Hereford and Durham, he suggested to the writer that the chapter should be expanded into a book which he would publish. Henson countered with the idea of a book on the history of English Nonconformity; Stedman accepted this but it was never written. However, he had now been badly bitten by the publishing bug, and began soliciting books from well-known authors. He received several rejections before two of them were prepared to accept him, an oddly assorted couple united by their prolificness: Edna Lyall, and the Reverend Sabine Baring-Gould, a vicar, a folk-song and tale collector and the father of a great many children and books, both fiction and non-fiction, whose *Songs of the West* is a classic of the English folk-dance and song revival, and whose most famous composition is the hymn 'Onward Christian Soldiers'. His *Mehalah* is still a readable and romantic novel, a *Tess of the D'Urbervilles* set in Essex with a splendidly tomboyish heroine who wears a fisherman's knitted cap.

The Methuen list therefore began appropriately with a stillborn whiff of theology, and with fiction. It is unclear why Stedman chose to call his new company Methuen, but perhaps he wished to keep the company name distinct from his authorial name. He rented a small back room at 19 Bury Street Bloomsbury from, rather unpromisingly, a remainder merchant, W.W. Gibbons, who was to be the new company's trade manager while Stedman continued to run his school and solicit new authors. In that first year he took back his textbooks and the book on Oxford from George Bell and Sons and so had the twin pillars of fiction and educational publishing to prop up his enterprise. It is good to note that the first book to bear the Methuen name was Edna Lyall's *Derrick Vaughan, Novelist,* so beginning Methuen's long association with and reliance on the work of writers who were women, many of whom have been and are concerned with what in the 1890s was known as 'the woman question' and is now called feminism.

Lyall, whose real name was Ada Ellen Bayly, was a polemical novelist, whose fiction was a vehicle for her political and philosophical convictions, which included women's emancipation, humanism and Home Rule for Ireland. Her subject matter was probably the source of the connection between Lyall and Stedman, for from the first, as well as the staples of education, theology and popular fiction, the list shows a strong bias

towards liberal humanist thinking in its *Early Public Life of William Ewart Gladstone* by A. F. Robbins, and the many-volume edition of his speeches, and in the fascinating series Social Questions of Today, which, by the appearance of the first catalogue in 1894, included books on trade unionism, the rural exodus, women's work, the co-operative movement and the industrial condition of the poor.

*Derrick Vaughan, Novelist,* which sold 25,000 copies in its first year, is also an appropriate header for the Methuen list because of its apologia for the novelist's life and its clear depiction of the mechanics of late nineteenth-century publishing. Derrick has a twin, the soldier Lawrence, the man of action and of military heroism juxtaposed with the heroism of pursuing a vocation, that of novelist, against all odds while nursing an alcoholic father. Writers of all periods can endorse Derrick's plea for understanding and recognition.

> 'Why is it,' he exclaimed, 'that every other profession can be taken seriously, but that a novelist's work is supposed to be mere play? Good God! don't we suffer enough? Have we not hard brain work and drudgery of desk work and tedious gathering of statistics and troublesome search into details? Have we not an appalling weight of responsibility upon us? – and are we not at the mercy of a thousand capricious chances?'

Edna Lyall

Vaughan is writing his first novel, *Lynwood's Heritage*, a classic three-parter for the circulating libraries which dominated the fiction market, a situation which Lyall, no doubt in company with other writers, found less than satisfactory. When Vaughan has a success with his second novel: 'Speedily a second edition was called for; then, after a brief interval, a third edition – this time a rational one-volume affair, and the whole lot – 6,000 I believe – went off on the day of publication.' *Derrick Vaughan, Novelist* itself was in its twenty-fourth thousand by the end of the first year, and a 'rational one-volume' edition.

The success of Vaughan's second novel *At Strife* comes when it has been rejected by six publishers. The seventh 'wrote a somewhat dubious letter: the book he thought had great merit but unluckily people were prejudiced, and historical novels rarely met with success. However, he was willing to take the story, and offered half profits, candidly admitting that he had no great hopes of a large sale.' Publication takes a very short time. From a manuscript reaching a publisher to a reader's report and acceptance is a month, and from the arrival of the proofs to publication is a month. Writers weren't expected then to submit two copies in typescript. Vaughan's book is handwritten on blue foolscap and of course this intensifies the 'odd feeling, that first seeing oneself in print' when the proofs come.

There's an interesting sidelight on the question of censorship by fathers of what daughters may read. Vaughan's first novel is attacked, quite unjustly, Lyall lets us believe, by a reviewer who suggests that the book is 'dangerous', and the girl Derrick loves is forbidden by her father to read it although it is in the house: 'he is very particular about what we read'.

The story is told by a male narrator, Derrick's friend and admirer, who presents an agnostic and cynical view of the world, heavily influenced by the rationalism of Herbert Spencer, while Vaughan himself has a low-key unpious practical Christianity. The relatively new science of heredity makes several appearances as an explanation for psychological or physical make-up. It's a pre-Freudian world, where the main evils are drink and vanity; Lyall doesn't here enter into a discussion of the 'new woman' or the poor, the two great topics of the day, but her heroine Freda embodies the growing independence of spirit which girls were exhibiting, and is described as being 'no bread-and-butter miss, content meekly to adore her fiancé and deem him faultless'.

Baring-Gould's fine contributions for the new company were two non-fiction volumes: *Old Country Life* and *Historic Oddities and Strange Events*, both belonging to a species of compilation which has largely died out: the anecdotal collection with a folklorist flavour, now invaluable to the social historian, since the material has disappeared in its living form because of greater literacy and the subsequent loss of continuity in our oral traditions.

By 1890 the business needed a second room and twenty books were published that year, but the first great success, as the founder saw it in an interview he gave to *The Sketch* in 1896, was the publication of Kipling's *Barrack-Room Ballads* in 1892.

> The disreputable lingo of Cockayne is henceforth justified before the world; for a man of genius has taken it in hand, and has shown, beyond all cavilling, that in its way it also is a medium for literature. You are grateful, and you say to yourself, half in envy and half in admiration: 'Here is a *book*; here or one is a Dutchman, is one of the books of the year.'

That was how the *National Observer* reviewed it while *The Times* spotted 'unmistakable genius' which 'rings in every line'.

Kipling's immediate appeal is, like that of John Betjeman, in his accessibility, but he also caught a mood of the times, a desire to believe in the strength of Britain as embodied in the qualities of those private soldiers who had fought in India and who were to fight the Boers, who themselves commanded, though often grudgingly, great admiration from much of the British public (including Stedman himself, whose short analysis of the whole saga, *Peace or War in South Africa*, was first published in 1901). The politicians might make a mess of things and the proliferation of empire bring huge problems to the national psyche, but the simple soldiers would hold the world together with a kind of honour:

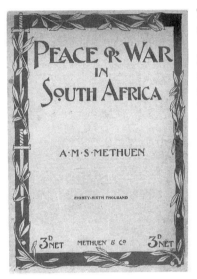

> For it's Tommy this, an' Tommy that, an' 'Chuck him out the brute!'
> But it's 'Saviour of 'is Country' when the guns begin to shoot.
> An' it's Tommy this, an' Tommy that, an' anything you please
> An' Tommy ain't a bloomin' fool – you bet that Tommy sees!

Kipling's elevation of dialect to poetry was a natural parallel to its accepted use in the work of Dickens and other prose writers. The influence of the music hall, the great popular medium for poetry and song recognised and valued by many writers, including Shaw, is also strong, both in the language and the form of the ballads.

Kipling's relationship with Methuen, however immediately profitable to them both, wasn't to include his prose. Before his next volume of verse, *The Seven Seas*, came out in 1896 he was already dallying with Macmillan for his children's prose work, *The Jungle Book. The Seven Seas*, though, contains several of his best and best-known poems: 'M'Andrew's Hymn', 'The Mary

Gloster', 'Sestina of the Tramp-Royal', 'The Sergeant's Wedding', 'The 'Eathen'.

Five years of solid growth had made the move from the remainder merchant's back rooms necessary and possible. A new manager, G. E. Webster from Kegan Paul, Trench, Trübner was appointed, and offices taken at 36 Essex Street in April 1894.

Yet in spite of the success of *Barrack-Room Ballads*, it was fiction which had built up the company. We have to think back to a world before television and film, before even radio, to gauge the true importance of novels to readers and therefore to the whole of the book trade. Popular novels went into several editions and could sell a hundred thousand or more copies in their lifespans. As well as sales to individual readers, there was the circulating library market of Mudies, W. H. Smith and Boots, who had been largely responsible for encouraging the development of the 400,000-word, three-decker novel. This was the literary equivalent of the broadcast soap, which appeals to some deep need in the human psyche for a continuing narrative, an alternative existence in the imagination in which the audience can immerse itself, as in sleep, for psychological renewal through an almost magical rite of empathy with mythical characters whose problems are still reflections of those of Greek drama in contemporary dress.

The Methuen list had soon attracted to itself some of the bestselling writers of the day, including Mrs Oliphant, now nearly at the end of a writing career which had covered forty-five years and nearly a hundred volumes, and the outseller of them all, Marie Corelli. Mrs Oliphant's *Sir Robert's Fortune*, published in 1895, two years before her death, received glowing reviews, especially for its descriptions of Highland scenery, an extended use of the pathetic fallacy to great effect and for its emotional insights. The story is set in Scotland before the Married Women's Property Act came into force, and Oliphant's contrast between the customs and mores of that earlier period and her modern times of universal gas lighting and railways point up the unexpressed parallel between that earlier condition of women as the chattels of their menfolk and the contemporary struggle for new legislation that would give them the full rights of suffrage.

> In those days there were no discussions of women's rights; but yet in those days, as in all other periods, the heart of a high-spirited young woman here and there swelled high with imaginative wrath, and indignation at the thought of those indignities which all women had to suffer. That it should be taken as a simple thing that any man, after he had gone through all the soils and degradations of a reckless life, should have a spotless girl given to him to make him a new existence, was one of those bitter thoughts that rankled in the minds of many women ...

The two women round whom the story centres embody different female responses to the demands of life and their male-dominated world. Helen Blythe believes that a woman has the power to save a man. In the end she is shown not to have saved exactly but to have 'pulled through' her wild lover. However, Lily, the heroine, feels only the impotence that is at odds with her intelligence and desire to act. She is the plaything of men, both uncle and husband, who make all the decisions and continue to treat her as a pretty child for their amusement and comfort, without the legislation that would make her an independent being, and without, Oliphant says unequivocally (who knew the bitterness of this truth in her own life), the power of money to set her free to act.

Marie Corelli's *A Romance of Two Worlds* had begun her fiction career in 1886. In 1893 Methuen published *Barabbas*, which was a runaway success, partly or perhaps largely because of the controversy it aroused. While the Christian press praised it, the secular damned it, accusing it, ironically, of blasphemy. Bad taste would have been a more rational, though

not so exciting, charge. In their note to the fifth edition in the first number of the *Methuen Gazette*, which the company began to publish on moving to their new premises, the publishers wrote:

> Few books in late years have received such savage and merciless treatment from the critics as Miss Corelli's latest romance. To re-produce the epithets which have been hurled at it would be to compile a dictionary of choice Billingsgate.... Meanwhile the public, indifferent to the voice of the critic, and to charges of blasphemy, crowds to the sale. The first large issue of the cheap edition and a second reprint were sold before publication, and an eighth edition is now nearly exhausted, so that there is still balm in Gilead.

The question of what was an edition exercised both publishers and writers. It's clear both from the same number of the *Methuen Gazette* and from Corelli's next amazing success, *The Sorrows of Satan*, that some publishers, in order to 'boom' a book, issued as many editions as possible. Methuen (almost certainly Stedman in person) frowned on this practice. 'To print say 750 copies of a novel and to divide this into five "editions" of 150 each, announcing the exhaustion of each puny infant with a prodigious flourish is ridiculous, and perhaps immoral. At all events it is meant to bamboozle the public.'

At the same time it was a highly competitive world, and one in which it was impossible to hang on to a successful but restless author. After the success of *Barabbas* Corelli's next book was with Methuen, and an even greater sale, but her 1896 publisher was Hutchinson with *The Mighty Atom*, a book which Methuen didn't acquire until 1906, twenty-five editions later. Unlike some of his contemporaries, Stedman insisted on date of publication and often a full publishing history appearing in all his books from the beginning of the company.

Then, as now, both writers and readers were fascinated by writing and publishing, a fascination which sometimes seems introverted and navel-gazing, but is clearly so well established that the public must at least be party to what might otherwise be thought purely a writerly obsession. *Derrick Vaughan, Novelist* is a clear case but *The Sorrows of Satan* is even stronger. Corelli herself appears in the book, along with Prince Lucio Rimanez – Satan, and a would-be novelist and millionaire whose soul is eventually saved by the Corelli figure, the bestselling author Mavis Clore.

It's Corelli's way of having her own back on the castigators of *Barabbas*. Satan contrives that the protagonist's novel shall succeed by all the current tricks of the trade, known as 'booming': the several small editions, the bullying and buying of critics. Meanwhile, having almost sold his soul to the devil, the protagonist, Geoffrey Tempest, writes an anonymous and swingeing attack on Mavis Clore's new book, out of envy of her success and because he hates 'women who write'. Even the devil is shocked.

> Why? Because they are able to exist independently? Would you have them all the slaves of man's lust or convenience? My dear Geoffrey, you are unreasonable. If you admit that you are jealous of this woman's celebrity and grudge it to her, then I can understand your spite, for jealousy is capable of murdering a fellow-creature with either the dagger or the pen.

Those who criticised Corelli had sold themselves to the devil, for she saw herself as an upholder of Christian beliefs and standards in an increasingly corrupt world that cared only for money and 'noisy notoriety'. Yet of course she had both herself. She speaks of the critics, who hardly earn a pound a week, regarding 'as their natural enemies the authors who make thirty to fifty pounds a week', a figure that must reflect her own earnings at this time.

Although a despised woman writer, Mavis Clore is 'as unlike the accepted ideal of the female novelist as she can well be', that is, 'an elderly, dowdy, spectacled, frowsy fright'. She is 'a quiet, graceful creature, so slight and dainty, so perfectly unaffected and simple in manner ... – she rather resembled a picture by Greuze in her soft white gown with a pale rose nestled amid the old Flemish lace at her throat – and as she turned her head towards us, the sunlight caught her fair hair and turned it into the similitude of a golden halo ...' Flattering self-portraiture can hardly ever have gone further.

At one point she complains that the 'Saturday' has said that she only wins the applause of shop girls and it's interesting to speculate on the source of her appeal. Nothing could be further from the rationalism of Lyall or the balanced insights of Oliphant. Corelli's novels are, however, as much written with a polemical purpose as those of her contemporaries. *The Mighty Atom* has an epigraph by the author pointing out the moral of the book which she dedicates 'To those self-styled progressivists who by precept and example assist the infamous cause of education without religion and ... are guilty of a worse crime than murder.' Perhaps in spite of her enormous sales, Stedman found this hard to stomach and was content to wait for *The Sorrows of Satan*. It seems hardly likely that this was what appealed to the 'shop girls'.

Bernard Shaw found Corelli's Satan not nearly wicked enough when the book was dramatised, but he makes a winning fantasy figure off the Mr Rochester or Darcy peg: aloof, handsome, satirical and seemingly immune to the attractions of women, a combination recognisable in many conventional

women's magazine heroes. The novel is punctuated by a series of set pieces belonging firmly to the long tradition of Gothic horror which stretches from medieval romance to Stephen King via Ann Radcliffe. Although Satan is impervious to the passions which he arouses in women, this only enhances the sado-masochistic eroticism which is the underlying web through which Corelli weaves a flattering portrait of herself, and has her literary vengeance on the critics who had despised her. While railing against 'the "New" woman . . . the self-degrading creatures who delineate their fictional heroines as wallowing in unchastity, and who write freely on subjects which men would hesitate to name,' Corelli nevertheless raised the emotional temperature to a lurid pitch of unsatisfied and therefore constantly itching desire which is simply that lust she so often condemns.

The most perceptive study of such a personality is itself a fiction: Elizabeth Taylor's *Angel*, published in 1957, which combined aspects of Corelli and Ethel M. Dell in the popular romantic novelist Angelica Deverell, the angel–devil axis of *The Sorrows of Satan*.

It's hard not to believe that the scholarly Stedman knew Corelli's work was, from the literary point of view, what it has several times been described as, tosh, or the word she herself quotes: 'twaddle'. Nevertheless, if a publishing house was to keep afloat, then, as now, it needed the bestseller to balance the new scientific work on electricity or astronomy, or the difficult play by the gloomy Ibsen (*Brand*, published by Methuen in translation as early as 1894, and claimed as the first English version, so beginning their long tradition of a modern drama list); or indeed obscure literary Americans like Henry James, whose volume of short stories *The Soft Side* Methuen first published in 1900, and who sold very badly, and Emily Dickinson, who appeared in 1905.

The market also dictated that a book, to fulfil its maximum sales, should appear in several different editions at different prices with different covers. By 1894 Methuen were publishing new novels in three volumes at thirty-one shillings and sixpence, in two volumes at twenty-one shillings, single-volume 'new and cheaper editions' at six shillings, three-and-sixpenny novels, and cloth-bound novels by 'popular' authors at half-a-crown. There was as great a range in the pricing of non-fiction, with popular science as low as two shillings and sixpence, while Baring-Gould's *The Deserts of Southern France* was in two heavily illustrated volumes, with the libraries in mind, at thirty-two shillings.

All this was about to change. Two perennial concerns of the book trade, the library market and the net book agreement, came to the forefront in 1894. A special December number of the *Gazette* in its 'Literary Notes' describes what is happening. Messrs Mudie and W. H. Smith and Sons have given notice in

(*clockwise*) Henrik Ibsen

Rudyard Kipling

Marie Corelli

# A·HOVSE·OF·POMEGRANATES

## BY·OSCAR·WILDE·

WITH·SIXTEEN·ILLVSTRATIONS·BY·JESSIE·M·KING·

METHUEN·AND·COY·LTD·  LONDON

a circular to the publishers that they are no longer prepared to buy the two- and three-volume novel at the old price. They have suggested four shillings a volume. The *Gazette* comments:

> It is evidently impossible for publishers to sell novels at a reduction of at least twenty per cent from the former nett price, and at the same time to pay authors their former royalties or prices. Nor does it seem likely that publishers or authors will look upon the profits possible under the new systems as a reasonable reward for the risks of production or the labours of writing.

As far as Methuen were concerned, the tradition of the three-decker which had sustained Dickens (or which he had sustained) was over. Its questionable validity as an art form couldn't survive the commercial knock. Two- and three-volume novels disappear almost at once from Methuen's lists to be replaced by the six-shilling single volume. Edna Lyall, of course, would have welcomed the change, and so, no doubt, did other writers who must have rejoiced at no longer having to pad for the required length. Even so, a standard novel was long by late twentieth-century requirements at 150,000 words, around 400 printed pages. As usual, the change was seen as a mixed blessing. It was felt that authors of limited appeal would be 'starved out of existence' and that first books would find it harder to get a publisher, both still only too familiar arguments whenever change is in the air. However, 'the steady growth of the reading public, and the widening popularity of fiction, now render it possible and even desirable to issue stories at once in a popular form, and to appeal directly to the public'.

The *Gazette* felt that booksellers would benefit and any improvement in their lot, then as now, must be welcome. (Sometimes the texts are so familiar it hardly seems as if they can belong to another century.) 'The almost universal adoption of the discount system has reduced the profits of a bookseller to a miserable point, and in many country towns he has to eke out his scanty livelihood by the sale of "fancy goods". The old-fashioned bookseller, who knew and loved books, and could descant upon the merits of his stock, is becoming as distinct [sic] as the great auk.' Even before the post-1945 growth of the free public library system, the British public had long been unaccustomed to buying and owning rather than borrowing books. Geoffrey Tempest's beautiful and rich wife Sybil in *The Sorrows of Satan* says as a matter of course that she never buys a novel, except those of Mavis Clore, but always gets them from Mudies.

*The Times* had apparently been lending its columns to those in favour of the discount system, three pence in the shilling off the published price, and the problem was far from solved, although in the end in 1916 publishers and booksellers were to

combine to support the cover charge in the net book agreement. Perhaps all this controversy decided Stedman to give up his teaching and concentrate solely on the firm, which he did in 1895. His immense personal interest in all matters, which even extended to the order in which the books appeared in the catalogues, was sometimes exercised from his home in the Surrey hills near Haslemere, where he continued to produce his textbooks, and to garden, when he wasn't in his barely furnished office in Essex Street, which had a 'plain serviceable carpet, a nice grandfather clock and no outstanding pictures', or so E. J. Taylor, who first reported for work in the trade department as a boy in August 1903, remembered.

Baring-Gould had been one of Stedman's first supporters in the new enterprise and he was rewarded by the accolade of his own separate list in the catalogue, a distinction given to few writers and which included by the end of the first decade only Corelli, Anthony Hope and Gilbert Parker. Both men and women, as Aphra Behn had put it two hundred years before: 'were forced to write for bread and not ashamed to own it'. The rewards were high for the successful but at the cost of constant industry. A book a year was the accepted rate and a two-year gap was cause for comment. Baring-Gould diversified into non-fiction: history, music, topography, biography, writing in the high Victorian manner, standing at a tall desk like a lectern. Corelli had a carefully arranged study, a cross between boudoir and shrine, where the muse might descend in comfort.

With such an enormous output it's not perhaps surprising that Baring-Gould and other non-fiction populists should have made errors of fact in their work, but it must be realised that their function included much of what is now covered by television documentary. The late nineteenth century was a time in which the British population was avid for knowledge. If people couldn't travel they could read about foreign parts, especially the more exotic parts of empire, or they could try to understand, or at least to harness for practical purposes, the new science and technology, especially the still comparatively recent phenomenon of electricity. This desire to understand, and therefore possess, all, was I believe, an important factor in the promotion of series publishing. In particular the recently literate could begin to build a library of uniform volumes, and Stedman understood and exploited the public wish for this. The 1898 'List' begins with eight pages of forthcoming titles and then presents the full catalogue under headings starting appropriately with Poetry, as both bestseller and the highest of art forms. *Belles Lettres* and Anthologies follow and include the new edition of Shakespeare's poems, Yeats's first *Anthology of Irish Verse*, W. E. Henley's *English Lyrics* and Robert Louis Stevenson's *Vailima Letters*, as well as classics like Congreve, Johnson and Burns. Many of the categories are still, of course, extant: History; Biography; Science and Technology; Phil-

Ernest Glanville's *The Kloof Bride* (1898)

osophy; Methuen's Commercial Series, à reflection of the continuing expansion of commerce and its workforce; and of course school textbooks and examination papers, either by Stedman himself or edited by him. Social Questions of Today covers both the social sciences and politics and was a quietly successful series, but the new University Extension Series was to be beaten by Dent's Everyman editions at a relatively cheaper price: one shilling for cloth-bound. For once Stedman, having correctly defined a need, had been too late and too dear for this rapidly growing market of self-educators. This failure was to help in the process by which a house begun by a schoolmaster, principally to take back the publishing of his own textbooks, was to become known chiefly for its fiction.

However, he correctly judged the price for another new venture: the sixpenny paperback, which began with two novels in 1899. It's worth quoting the announcement in the *Gazette* in full.

> Messrs Methuen contemplate a very interesting experiment in publishing. They are about to issue, at Sixpence, under the general title of 'Methuen's Library of Fiction', stories by some of the best-known writers of the day. A few books will be reprints, but most will be new books hitherto unpublished in book form.
>
> A considerable number of sixpenny editions of old books have already been issued by various publishers, but in no case has the work of an author of high repute been published in the first instance at that price. This Messrs Methuen will attempt; and the first book thus published will be a New Novel by E. W. Hornung. Mr Robert Barr and Mr Cutcliffe Hyne will follow, and later will be published books by Mr Baring-Gould and others. In some cases the same book will be published simultaneously both at sixpence and at a higher price. Messrs Methuen recognise the inevitable tendencies of an age of cheap literature. The theatre has its stalls and its pit, the railway its first and its third classes; so the novelist may well have a double audience, and while the wealthy will still pay six shillings for their novels, those of limited means may be able to purchase the same book in a decent but less luxurious form.

In fact, this enterprise soon became the monthly publication which by 1902 already included thirty-two titles. In the same year it was supplemented by Methuen's Sixpenny Library, which was to include 'great and popular books of past years' like *Ben Hur*, *Cranford*, *The Mill on the Floss* and *Peter Simple*. All these sixpenny publications were aimed at 'a large class of readers who are somewhat weary of the average magazine, who cannot buy a six-shilling novel or subscribe to a library,

15

and who enjoy a healthy story full of incident or pathos or humour'. The apologia is an interesting mixture of philanthropy and commerce, designed to combat the old argument that more means worse. Many had feared that it might 'open the floodgates to vulgarity and strike a deadly blow at the six-shilling novel', thereby affronting public taste and the trade's profits in one go.

Baring-Gould's own novels were certainly full of incident, pathos and humour. *In the Roar of the Sea* is a typical product, and one of Methuen's earliest successes. He is always strong on place, using the landscapes where he had been a vicar and a knowledge of people of all classes, their dialects and songs, obtained from the same source. There is usually, in deference to his women readers, a well-defined heroine, sometimes a tomboy, perhaps with elements of the millgirl he took and educated to be his wife in his first Essex parish, where *Mehalah*, his best-known novel, is set, or the equally strong-minded, though very feminine and cultured, Judith of *In the Roar of the Sea*, a vicar's daughter who is perhaps modelled on one of his own.

The male protagonist is frequently an anti-hero, another of the wild macho characters that might be reclaimed by the love of a good women, or might instead destroy her. In the earlier book Mehalah is drowned by her lover but by *In the Roar of the Sea* Judith is allowed to survive, with intimations of possible future happiness after cruel Coppinger has chosen death by fire. The heroine, if she survives, is often saved by the 'good' male character. It's as though the late Victorian psyche is positing a deliberately ambiguous male in separating out the two halves of a personality which represent aggression and passion, with their darker face of violence and intimidation, and security and gentleness, with the possibility of attendant weakness.

Even in another and very different bestseller, *Dodo* by E. F. Benson, where the backdrop isn't the conventionally romantic wild grandeur of the Cornish coast but polite and witty upper-class society, the heroine is won by the domineering, calculating Prince Waldenach, while the amiable and caring Jack is abandoned. It's hard to know what to think of the heroine herself, Dodo, who is a tease and a rattle, refusing to take anything seriously except her own diversion. The dialogue is sub-Wildean, a fictive comedy of manners which nevertheless concerns itself with those social and psychological problems that were the immediate issues of the day.

So too does Anthony Hope's bestseller, *The God in the Car*, which brings together several late Victorian obsessions. Hope is of course chiefly known for *The Prisoner of Zenda* and its sequel *Rupert of Hentzau*, which, especially as processed by Hollywood, have given him the reputation of a swashbuckler, but his preoccupation is with internal adventures, not external action. Adultery deeply concerned both the individual and the

collective social conscience, and especially, perhaps because more women read fiction, the female conscience. Maggie of *The God in the Car* falls desperately in love with Willie Ruston, the embodiment of that god in the exorable car of progress which bruises and breaks lesser people under its wheels. In the end she decides to stay with the husband who loves her because she sees that Willie's true allegiance is to his project, his work and ambition, and that is really why she loves him. She admires his strength and drive and realises that she doesn't want him to waver, even for her.

The project introduces another nineteenth-century concern reflected in several titles in the Methuen list: Africa. Ruston is an empire-builder and from one side appears a ruthless charlatan. The implication is that without this kind of undaunted capitalism the car doesn't go forward but that it's at the expense of the victims: African natives, women and young men eager for adventure. The book, therefore hides under a tailored morning coat the dual problem of what men and women respectively should do when confronted by the challenge of the car. Ruston's flirtation with Maggie causes havoc for her, her husband and their friends, and had it gone any further would have upset her children, who are, as it is, made very uneasy by the relationship. Yet is he simply an egocentric bounder or are his ruthlessness and power a necessary force of history, an evolutionary drive which ensures the survival of the fittest?

A BOOK OF
CHRISTMAS VERSE

SELECTED BY H. C. BEECHING: WITH
TEN DESIGNS BY WALTER CRANE

LONDON: METHUEN AND COMPANY
36 ESSEX ST: STRAND: MDCCCXCV

The novelists between them exhibit a full range of the available literary pre-modernist styles, from the rhetoric of Corelli at one extreme, via the cultured, well-modulated tones of Anthony Hope, to the demotic realism of Arthur Morrison, probably the most considerable of the British prose writers of Methuen's early years before H. G. Wells joined the list in 1897 with a volume of short stories, *The Plattner Story and Others*. Arthur Morrison's reputation rests on two of his books which deal with the East End of London, an area almost as exotic and fascinating to the Victorian reader as Africa itself, and filled with savage natives with a language and customs barbaric enough to be studied. Like Africa, it too had its missionaries, one of whom was Morrison's friend Arthur Jay, vicar of Shoreditch, who figures in the novel *A Child of the Jago*, which is dedicated to him and which followed the very successful collection *Tales of Mean Streets*, most of the stories from which had been published in the *Pall Mall Budget*, the *National Observer* or *Macmillan's Magazine*.

The *National Observer* was edited by another Methuen author, or rather editor, W. E. Henley, to whom *Tales from Mean Streets* is dedicated. Henley, a friend of R. L. Stevenson, model for Long John Silver, champion of Whistler, editor of among others Henry James, Yeats, Kipling and H. G. Wells (all or some of whom he may have brought to the Methuen list), and himself a prolific poet, was a defender of realism and an editor of *Slang*

*and Its Analogues*, both of which would have given him great sympathy for Morrison.

Morrison himself, however, in an afterword to the February 1897 edition of *A Child of the Jago*, professed himself uneasy with the 'realist' label, insisting that he is 'a simple writer of tales, who takes whatever means lie to his hand to present life as he sees it'. He goes on:

> I have been asked, in print, if I think that there is no phase of life which the artist may not touch. Most certainly I think this. . . . It is the artist's privilege to seek his material where he pleases, and it is no man's privilege to say him nay. If the community have left horrible places and horrible lives before his eyes, then the fault is the community's and to picture these places and these lives becomes not merely his privilege but his duty.

These two books are by Dickens out of Mayhew's *London Labour and the London Poor*. Their dialogue is in a language which persisted until after the Second World War and traces of it are still preserved in the popular television soap opera *EastEnders*, as well as in those lyrics of Chas and Dave which are modelled on music-hall songs. Some of it is thieves' cant but a major part of it formed a working-class sub-language which turns up in Flora Thompson's rural speakers as well as in the Jago. Even though the pronunciation was different, much of the vocabulary and syntax were common to all parts of England.

Morrison doesn't sentimentalise his characters. To those critics who had suggested that he should only write about the Jago 'ever weeping', he replied that he refused 'to weep obscenely in the public gaze. In other words that I shall do their weeping for them as a sort of emotional bedesman: that I shall make public parade of sympathy in their behalf so that they may keep their sympathy for themselves, and win comfort from the belief that they are eased of their just responsibility by vicarious snivelling.' He is often tough on his characters, writing of the 'mean cunning' that 'saw a mystery and a terror where simple intelligence saw there was none'. The people of the Jago are filthy, violent, lying, stupid, everything that can be called vicious or criminal, yet they remain human and tragic because their evils are perpetuated by history and society. The Jago isn't one small street but

> only a link in a long and mightily tangled chain – is only a turn in a tortuous maze. This street of the square holes is hundreds of miles long. That it is planned in short lengths is true, but there is no other way in the world that can more properly be called a single street, because of its dismal lack of accent, its sordid uniformity, its utter remoteness from delight.

The people of the street are unlikely to recognise themselves in the books for 'Nobody reads poetry or romance. . . . A Sunday paper in some few houses provides such reading as this street is disposed to achieve. Now and again a penny novel has been found among the treasures of a growing daughter, and has been wrathfully confiscated. For the air of this street is unfavourable to the ideal.'

If anything, Morrison could be accused of being too harsh with his characters and holding them up to ridicule, but the death of the child of the Jago, Dicky Perrot, and the execution of his father belie this charge, as too that other of exploiting the characters and their world for a kind of picaresque black humour. In 1899 he was to receive an accolade given to few writers when the then Prince of Wales, soon to be Edward VII, opening the new County Council buildings at Shoreditch 'made a strongly appreciative reference to *A Child of the Jago*; the only occasion, it is said, on which His Majesty has taken public notice of the work of a living novelist', the *Gazette* reported, continuing in its 1901 literary notes:

> A few weeks ago the library of HMS Ophir was sold by auction at Stevens' rooms and it was then seen that in the copy of *Tales of Mean Streets*, which was one of the very few volumes of fiction selected to travel round the world with the Prince and Princess of Wales, His Royal Highness had written, against the tale 'Lizerunt', the remark: 'This is very powerful. – George.'

In spite of this, Stedman was perhaps relieved when Morrison's next East End novel, *To London Town*, could be described as 'more idyllic in its surroundings and more optimistic in its outlook', but perhaps that is why it's now unknown.

By 1897 Stedman was making enough money from publishing to rebuild his house, Honey Hanger, near Haslemere as New Place and to employ Charles Voysey and Gertrude Jekyll to redesign the garden, twenty largely wild acres with only a kitchen garden and a small space for his favourite alpines. Already by 1896 Stedman was claiming to do most of his work in the country, though this seems from E. J. Taylor's account to be a little exaggerated, since he spent mid-week in London and then was driven to Waterloo Station in a four-wheeler to catch the train back to Surrey. When he wasn't in London an office boy had the task of buying and posting him copies of the *Westminster Gazette* and the *Pall Mall Gazette*, and a lengthy account of the day's happenings was also sent, which came back by return, such was the postal service a hundred years ago, 'with clear indications of the course of action to be followed in every matter'. He had married in 1884 Emily Caroline, daughter of a London solicitor, Edwin Bedford, whose brother, also Edwin, was ordained curate of Haslemere after taking his

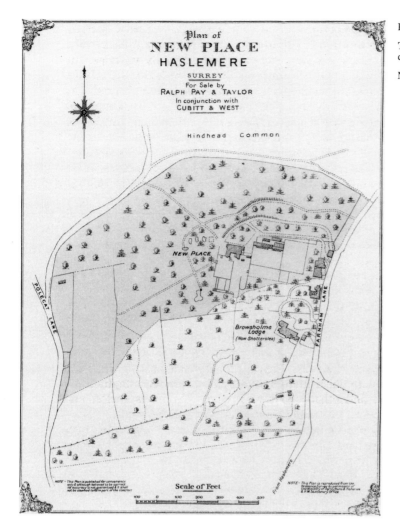

Plan of New Place, Haslemere

The garden at New Place,
designed by Gertrude Jekyll

New Place, Haslemere

degree at Cambridge in 1884, though whether he was given the post through his brother-in-law Stedman's influence it's hard to tell. There were to be no children of this marriage, but they shared a love of gardening, and the gardens at New Place were opened to the public every year after the First World War, though when the annual staff outing visited Haslemere in 1913, tea had to be taken at a hotel in Hindhead for fear of damage to the lawns and formal flower beds.

*In the Roar of the Sea* by Baring-Gould itself throws an interesting sidelight on children's books. Describing Judith's room, Baring-Gould, who knew all about such things as a prolific parent and writer, says rather tartly, speaking of a child's books of ninety years before: 'Books for children were rare in those days, and such as were produced were read and re-read until they were woven into the very fibre of the mind, never more to be extricated and cast aside. Now it is otherwise. A child needs a story-book every week, and each new story-book effaces the impression produced by the book that went before.'

Stedman, too, must have realised from his own teaching experience that there was a large children's market to be supplied, and Methuen were quickly into the field. By the time of the first extant full list in 1898 there is something for every age-group. There are heavily illustrated books for the very young with illustrations by Walter Crane, the Birmingham Art School, and others: nursery rhymes, Christmas verses, and three books by Baring-Gould himself of fairy tales and more nursery songs and rhymes. Two other series – Books for Boys and Girls and The Peacock Library, which was specifically for girls – have titles by L. T. Meade and Mrs Molesworth; a romance for children by Baring-Gould, *The Icelander's Sword*; and Methuen's first children's humorous fantasy in the Lewis Carroll tradition, the Wallypug series by G. E. Farrow. The first children's book to be published seems to have been L. T. Meade's *A Girl of the People*, which is a teenage romance for girls and is first mentioned in the out letter book in February 1890. *The Red Grange* by Molesworth and *The Secret of Madame de Monluc* by the mysterious 'Miss Roberts', who always appeared pseudonymously as the author of Mademoiselle Mori, soon followed. The first books for younger children were *Only a Guard-Room Dog* by Edith E. Cuthall and *The Doctor of the Juliet* by Harry Collingwood, which was specifically aimed at boys. Presumably, as they grew older male persons were meant to move on to non-fiction, as there's nothing comparable to The Peacock Library for them. Girls, however, had to be protected from reading anything improper, and so special provision was made for books which parents could feel easy about their daughters reading. The double standard paved the way for Angela Brazil.

Baring-Gould's *The Icelander's Sword* is intended for boys; he had first written it in 1858, but his instinct that it would still please boys thirty-six years later seems to have been justified,

for it stayed in the children's list for many years after its re-publication in 1894, in an edition which incorporated the revisions he was able to make after a visit to Iceland in 1861. The language of this, as well as that of other children's books of the period, seems now to be without concession to the limitations of a youthful vocabulary, and the girls' books are full of passion, violence and strong emotions, unlike the school stories which were to replace them after the First World War; indeed, a letter from Methuen attempting to sell the colonial rights in several of the *Peacock* series says of *The Red Grange* 'this is *not* a juvenile book'.

The first bestseller, however, in what was to be a line that would stretch through Toad and Pooh to Babar and Tintin, was the series by G. E. Farrow about the ineffectual King Wally-pug and his royal suite, and it brought its inventor the unmistakable accolade of being written to by children from all over the world clamouring for more. Like Kipling, G. E. Farrow was agented by A. P. Watt, and like him, too, he was inclined to change publishers and therefore had his correspondence directed to his agent. There was of course no separate children's department in the firm and Stedman oversaw these books along with all the rest.

Children's books depend heavily on illustration, but many of the adult novels too were illustrated with at least a frontispiece. Alan Wright provided the later drawings for the Wallypug series, while Walter Crane and the students of the Birmingham Art School contributed to other heavily illustrated anthologies, but Methuen's chief illustrator was Francis Bedford, whose early work has great Art Nouveau charm. With the turn of the century and the publication of E. V. Lucas's *The Visit to London*, his work becomes more naturalistic without losing its original freshness and appeal.

E. V. Lucas, who was eventually to become chairman of the company after Stedman's death, was first brought in by the poet and editor H. C. Beeching, who had already edited two anthologies for Methuen. Himself a good poet and a friend of W. E. Henley, Beeching formed part of a *belles lettres* group of Methuen authors and editors which included Henry James and R. L. Stevenson, and gave the list literary respectability to balance the bestsellers, with Kipling's poetry straddling the two ends of the publishing spectrum. It must have been Henley who brought Kipling to Stedman to give the firm its first runaway success in 1892, less than three years after its founding.

Henley was editor of the *National Observer* during the company's first years and gave several Methuen authors their first exposure in print, including Kipling, Kenneth Grahame, Gilbert Parker and Arthur Morrison. His co-editor was Charles Whibley, who also collaborated with him on an anthology of English prose for Methuen in 1894. His brother Leonard, who shared a house with Charles and Henley and was himself a classicist, joined Methuen in 1890 as a 'partner' to the remainder merchant W. W. Gibbings, who was the trade manager, presumably to help Stedman with the editorial side. A. P. Watt sent them the Kipling manuscript early in January 1892. Times seem to have been a little hard, and the company had been forced to offer reduced terms to the circulating libraries for three-decker novels in order to attract more custom. They expected from the beginning a big sale in India for *Barrack-Room Ballads*. It's interesting, and cheering, to find them in June 1892 in a letter to a G. F. Cobb who wanted to publish six of the poems in what must have been an American magazine, resisting a bowdlerisation of 'Fuzzy Wuzzy': 'We think that people to whom the song would appeal would not be offended by the *damn*: whereas the change you propose seems to us out of tune with the poem, and therefore weak.'

Whibley seems to have embarked either in his own or the firm's capacity on the publication of a magazine, *Literary Opinion*, which only lasted a few months before one of the other backers withdrew and the enterprise had to be wound up. Perhaps this failure had something to do with Whibley's leaving and retiring to Yorkshire, where he continued to be a reader for the firm. His replacement, George Webster, had already had sixteen years with Kegan Paul, Trench, Trübner – Stedman's own first publisher. He was very experienced in the business and addresses A. P. Watt at once as 'Mr Watt', and within weeks as 'My dear Watt' when 'Dear Sir' was the norm.

Watt often seems to have acted as go-between in sales of American rights, especially with Houghton Mifflin. Both sheets and rights were sold and Methuen, presumably Stedman himself, preferred to keep the English method of spelling. The out letter book for this period, unfortunately the only one to survive, is full of such glimpses of the early day-to-day running of the company, including copies of letters of rejection to authors, the terms of which still have a familiar ring. Methuen had two methods of publication. When they really wanted a work, especially from a known author, they offered a royalty of 10 per cent on the first 500 copies and thereafter $12\frac{1}{2}$ per cent, sometimes rising even higher, though Gilbert Parker, who was to become one of their most popular novelists, only rose to $12\frac{1}{2}$ per cent after 1,500 on his first book. When there were doubts about the book they would often offer to publish on a commission basis, charging a fee of £10 and paying 10 per cent on the sales. A thousand copies cost roughly £50 for paper and print and fourpence or fivepence a copy for binding. In some cases a royalty was withheld on the first 250 copies to recover the costs on an unknown author.

Frequently the reason given for rejecting a manuscript was that the genre, poetry, sacred novels, short stories, historical novels, were 'rarely successful from a commercial point of view'. 'Sacred novels are rarely if ever successful for obvious

reasons', one hopeful was told; *Barabbas* hadn't yet appeared on the scene. 'Poetry', in spite of Kipling, 'seldom pays', Alexander Stuart had to read when he submitted his *Ballads of the North*.

What did seem to pay was theology, and here is the greatest difference between the lists of today and a hundred years ago. By 1898 Methuen were publishing four series: Handbooks of Theology, The Churchman's Library (which included two books by Hensley Henson, who may be said to have provoked the whole enterprise, and, interestingly in view of the continued controversy about the ordination of women, a book on *The Ministry of Deaconesses*), The Library of Devotion, and Leaders of Religion, edited by H. C. Beeching, who was himself a clergy-man and curate in the parish of Yattendon where Robert Bridges, whose niece he had married, was choirmaster. E. V. Lucas records that the two poets fell out over the division of the service and Bridges led the choirboys out in the middle of it one Sunday, never to return but thereafter to stand at the gate urging parishioners not to go in.

Clergymen were educated but impoverished and the list reflects this, as well as the period's deep absorption in the Christian Church and Stedman's own clerical connections. In 1897 Methuen became the sole suppliers of books, their own and others' publications, to the Book Grant Society, which supplied 'good readable books' to parish libraries, workhouses 'and other deserving and charitable institutions'. It's unlikely that the *Barrack-Room Ballads* or *Tales of Mean Streets* were among them, or indeed, but in this instance for reasons of price, Methuen's two non-fiction bestsellers: Flinders Petrie's *A History of Egypt* in six volumes (though some of his cheaper books on Egypt may have been) and W. G. Collingwood's *Life of John Ruskin*. From the perspective of twenty-three years later, these were two of the works singled out for praise by an anonymous commentator. There is almost an attempt to produce something as grand as the Valley of the Kings itself in Flinders Petrie's heavily illustrated records of a buried civi-lisation that so touched the high Victorian imagination; while the homage to Ruskin was described in a review as 'one of the most beautiful books about one of the noblest lives of our century'.

The century and Methuen's first decade were drawing to a close, but there were two more literary events to come: the Arden Shakespeare, which followed the publication of an anno-tated edition of all the poems, and two books by H. G. Wells, who belongs unmistakably to the twentieth century, although Methuen published their first book of his stories, *The Stolen Bacillus*, in 1895 – stories which were said by the *Morning Post* to be 'far above the vast mass of tales which feed the popular craving for condensed fiction'.

Shakespeare's *Sonnets* appeared in 1898 edited by George Wyndham, who had previously edited North's *Plutarch*. In

(*left*) Sabine Baring-Gould

(*right*) R. L. Stevenson

1899, at the same time as it announced the sixpenny paperback novel, the *Gazette* trailered 'an edition of the works of Shakespeare in single plays. Professor Dowden, who is probably the most distinguished Shakespearean scholar living, has consented to act as general editor, and the first play thus produced will be "Hamlet" edited by Professor Dowden himself.' The series might well have foundered, for Dowden died after adding *Romeo and Juliet*, but it was saved by W. J. Craig, whose first contribution was *King Lear*.

Another literary monument was the complete Charles Dickens, edited with notes and illustrations by George Gissing, whose *The Town Traveller* Methuen had published the previous year to the relief of reviewers, who found that surprisingly it left 'no kind of bad taste in the mouth, no sense of the unutterable possibilities of washed-out dullness that lies, say, west of Hampstead Road'.

The last years of the century were those of economic depression, and then 'no trade', the *Gazette* wrote, 'suffers more acutely than the book industry. The average Englishman is not, under the most favourable circumstances, an extravagant book buyer, and a straitened income is felt in the library sooner than in the stables or the cellar.' Nevertheless the new company thrived, increasing the number of its titles and inventing new series every year. Yet if there can be said to be one author to

whom the endeavour owed its success it must be, I think, not Kipling, although he is the one who has passed into myth and history as the great sustainer, but the Reverend Sabine Baring-Gould, now forgotten except by folklorists. He is said to have been a friend of Stedman's and it was his promise of support that, along with Edna Lyall's, had started the whole thing off. The promise was kept, and by 1899 he had twenty-nine titles in the list, one of the most interesting of which, the novel *The Broom Squire*, must have been suggested by Stedman himself and is set in and around Hindhead within walking distance of his home, New Place.

Baring-Gould, the *Gazette* wrote, had never bowed the knee to the 'erotic, neurotic, and Tommyrotic' and had 'more imagination in his little finger than is contained in the whole horde of those young ladies and gentlemen who write nastiness and mistake it for genius'. His true genius, though forced by popular demand into the form of fiction, is that peculiarly Victorian blend arising from a fascination with the natural world, of fact and poetic description which has been largely superseded by the camera. though it has recently had a resurgence through a renewed interest in travel writing.

By 1899 it must have been clear that Algernon and his wife, Emily, had little hope of children. The firm, its books and authors, must have become a substitute for them. This would account for E. J. Taylor's comment that Stedman expected his employees to be loyal, and for his offering them shares in the company – which would as a general rule only be expected from a father to his children. All this must have been unconsciously if not consciously in his mind when, to celebrate the first decade of the house, he took its name for his own and became Algernon Methuen.

# TWO

# *The Georgians*
## 1899–1914

It would perhaps be comforting if history fitted neatly into decades or even centuries, but it has to be said that the coming of the twentieth century made little obvious immediate difference to Methuen's catalogue of authors. The popular fiction writers wrote on as busily as ever and were read as fervently. Marie Corelli produced her lamentation for the death of Queen Victoria and, almost as if she were replacing her, a Christmas message of exhortation and cheer. Certainly she saw, as others did, 'The Passing of the Great Queen as the commencement of a new era', but for the moment her publishers' first response, perhaps reflecting the Methuens', as they now were, own taste, was the introduction of a gardening list with *A Garden Diary* by one of their most prolific authors, the Hon. Emily Lawless, and *The British Gardener* by W. Williamson, 'a well-known expert'.

The nation's chief preoccupation was with the Boer War, still dragging on with more and more of the public sickened by it, and the list reflected this concern. So too did Corelli.

> Lift up thine eyes, Queen-Warrior of the world!
> Stand, fearless-footed on Time's shifting verge,
> And watch thy New Year's doubtful Dawn emerge
> From parting clouds thick-roll'd in thunderous War!

However, a couple of time-bombs which signalled the shape of things to come were ticking away in the list in H. G. Wells and Henry James. To turn from Corelli and Baring-Gould to Wells is to move from high Victorian rhetoric, deriving ultimately from the pulpit, to the language of democracy and science. Both Wells and James first appeared in the nineteenth century. Indeed, James had published *Daisy Miller* as early as 1879 and by 1895 was feeling unwanted by the public: 'A new generation that I know not, and mainly prize not, has taken universal possession. The sense of being utterly out of it, weighed me down, and I asked myself what the future would be,' he wrote to William Dean Howells. The truth is that he was before, or perhaps out of, his time. Frank Swinnerton, in his *Georgian Literary Scene*, suggests that James was the first

writer in English to see himself as an artist. This conception set him apart from the mainstream of his early contemporaries, whose motives in writing were either to make a living or in some sense to educate by means of a narrative. Incidentally, they expressed much more of their and their society's unconscious preoccupations than they realized, but they didn't compose a work of fiction in the conscious way that visual artists or symphonists do and had done for years. It was the study of Turgenev and Balzac as well as of the visual arts of Paris and London that gave James his idea of the novel as art, an idea which belongs essentially to one strand of modernist practice: the elevation of style to at least an equal place with content.

Both E. J. Taylor and a later chairman, J. Alan White, make it clear in their memoirs of the firm that Algernon Methuen himself governed editorial policy, seeking out new authors and devising new series. The magazines were still a fertile ground for new talent. Methuen himself was to write later to T. S. Eliot after seeing some of his unsigned articles on literary criticism in the *Times Literary Supplement*, and the result was *The Sacred Wood*, published in 1920. In the early part of the century the Café Royal was still a meeting place for writers where gossip and introductions could be exchanged. E. V. Lucas became a reader and editor with his own shared desk at Essex Street early in the new century after editing Lamb's *Essays of Elia* for H. C. Beeching's Little Library series. As Lucas himself said later in *Reading, Writing and Remembering*: 'Everything in life is linked.' Following this first commission in 1900, Methuen asked him to do a new complete edition and biography of Lamb.

In those days the population of the British Isles was half what it is a hundred years later, and the part of it that was educated and in membership of 'the profession of letters' was very small indeed. The more leisurely pace of life, at a time when even the most modestly published writer could afford some domestic help, gave opportunities for lunches, visits, conversation and correspondence. Lucas records innumerable meals and meetings whose cast lists read like an index to contemporary literature. His first encounter with another Methuen author, Conrad, is typical: 'It was one evening in 1895 that in the Restaurant d'Italia in Old Compton Street Edward Garnett beckoned to me from another table, and when I joined him introduced the friend with him as Mr Conrad, a ship's captain who had written a novel.' The book, *Almayer's Folly*, was lying in a roll of Fisher Unwin galley proofs on the table and Conrad had been encouraged to write it by John Galsworthy, a friend of Edward Garnett, with whom of course we are on the brink of Bloomsbury itself. Conrad had met Galsworthy, not then a writer, when he took a sea-trip on the *Torrens*, a sailing ship whose chief officer was Conrad.

Methuen first published him in 1906 with *The Mirror of the*

*Sea*, but he had solicited him as early as February 1899, when Conrad pleaded his slowness and obligations to other publishers for not being able to promise Methuen a book. He calls Methuen's 'a generous offer'. His books sold poorly, with print numbers of 3,000 and first bindings of 1,750, until the surprise success of *Chance* in 1914. Methuen continued to believe in him and promote his work in the announcement lists, which he always drew up personally, giving Conrad consistent billing near the top for nearly a decade with only a modest financial return.

Writers had no more brand loyalty then, it seems, than now. Kipling gave his prose to Macmillan; Wells at least offered his earlier works to Methuen, who announced the acquisition of *Love and Mr Lewisham*, *The Invisible Man*, *Tales of Space and Time* and *When the Sleeper Wakes* in 1903, but they mysteriously failed to appear. 1902 hadn't been a good year for books. The public was spending its money on the Jubilee, and great national events are, as the *Bulletin* noted rather sourly, rarely good for publishing sales. Conrad mentioned 'the general slump in the trade' in 1903 in a letter to Ford Madox Hueffer, later to become better known as Ford Madox Ford, who was, like Conrad, of European descent and therefore perhaps close to him, though not as affectionately addressed as 'Dear Jack' Galsworthy.

In spite of the book-trade depression, Methuen felt sufficiently confident to name The Arden Shakespeare and to announce what was another large enterprise: E. V. Lucas's edition of Lamb. Series were immensely popular, both with the public and the publisher. If the punters could be persuaded to begin collecting them, the chances were that they would go on indefinitely. 1904 saw the start of several of these ventures, from the highly priced – at twelve guineas the set of four – Shakespeare facsimile folios, subscribers to pay on delivery, to the new sixpenny paperbacks of Dumas's novels in a new translation 'by Mr Alfred Allison, whose competence is unquestioned, and he is assisted by a group of able scholars'. Long books were to be in double or treble volumes and there was also a superior cloth-bound, illustrated edition at prices from one shilling and sixpence to three and sixpence. Methuen says that he conceived this plan during the Dumas centenary in 1902. So popular were series that in 1905 the catalogue even offered a miniature revolving bookcase for ten shillings to keep your Little Quarto Shakespeares in.

The great innovation in series, however, was to be Methuen's Universal Library. Both as a good Liberal and as an ex-schoolmaster, he must have cherished the idea of reprinting the classics 'pure and unabridged ... only changed in so far that the antique spelling and punctuation have been discarded in favour of the modern', and especially under the general editorship of Sidney Lee, editor of the *Dictionary of National*

Methuen's Standard Library logo

*Biography* (which E. V. Lucas carried in its India-paper edition everywhere he went, in specially made portable cases). The *Bulletin* described the new sixpenny series as: 'This extraordinary enterprise which ... will be worthy of the suffrages of the rich as well as the support of the poor.'

Even before publication of the first volumes the title was changed to Methuen's Standard Library. 'Now many excellent books are being produced at sixpence but this is practically the first time you have been able to buy for this coin such books.... Thus when fifty volumes have been published, you will have a shelf-full of the finest literature of the world for under thirty shillings. Here is indeed the Poor Man's University.'

The great and the good hastened to send their support. The Archbishop of Canterbury thought 'these endeavours characteristic of our time, to make the masterpieces of English literature available even to those who have little money at their disposal for the purchase of books'. Lord Spencer wished Methuen success in their 'patriotic effort'. All the great educational authorities of the day, Winston Churchill, Sir Henry Campbell-Bannerman, the Bishop of Winchester and the Abbot Gasquet sent 'letters containing words equally warm'.

There's a mystery about the progress of the Standard Library. Both E. J. Taylor and Alan White agree that it was a flop, indeed White gives it only eighteen months, but it was still going in the last year of full publication before the First World War. Further, White implies that it was because Dent's Everyman volumes were only a shilling cloth-bound that they were more successful. But Methuen published simultaneously in paperback at sixpence and cloth-bound with gilt lettering at a shilling. It almost seems as if history has been revised by hindsight, and as though it was the war itself which put an end to this enterprise.

Winston Churchill's endorsement may owe something to Methuen's publication in 1905 of his biography of A. M. Scott. It was trailered in remarkably glowing terms to which hindsight, this time, gives an ironical gloss:

> If the fates are kind, there is little doubt but that a young man who celebrated his thirtieth birthday last December will be in a year to come Prime Minister of England.... He has genius and character, the gift of inspiration, and the power of bending others to his will. He is afraid of no one and nothing, he is a brilliant maker of phrases ...

It was to take two World Wars, thirty-five years and a change of party, which would have grieved Methuen himself bitterly, for this prophecy to be fulfilled.

1904 had been a financial success for the firm, with two popular hits: Robert Hichens's *The Garden of Allah* and Corelli's new novel blockbuster *God's Good Man*.

*(opposite clockwise)*
Joseph Conrad

Henry James

G. K. Chesterton

Robert Hichens

Depression may reign in the book trade and the purse of the burdened taxpayer be very light but everyone has enough money to buy Miss Corelli's new romance. And so edition after edition has been exhausted, and even the critics, not always generous to the distinguished author, have been forced to lay down their stilettos and admire.

Methuen once confessed to E. J. Taylor that he published the mediocre in order to be able to publish the things he valued, mentioning in particular the facsimile reprints of the Connoisseur's Library. He was obviously both knowledgeable and passionate about painting and sculpture, and the list reflects this in its wide range from Celtic art to Francesco Guardi, and in the series Little Books on Art and The Little Galleries.

*The Garden of Allah* had reached twenty-two editions by 1913, and it had become fashionable to hold 'Garden of Allah' parties in which, presumably, the guests dressed and behaved in Egyptian style or what passed for it after Hichens, who was really the male Corelli, in his lushness and eroticism tinged with sexual religiosity. The book's heroine, Domini, leaves dreary England after the death of her father in search of

> freedom, a wide horizon, the great winds, the great sun, the terrible spaces, the glowing, shimmering radiance, the hot, entrancing moons and bloomy purple nights of Africa. She wanted the nomads' fires and the acid voices of the Kabyle dogs. She wanted the roar of the tom-toms, the clash of the cymbals, the rattle of the negroes' castanets, the fluttering painted fingers of the dancers. She wanted – more than she could express, more than she knew.

This longing of Domini's could only have evoked such a response in British readers if it reflected a longing of their own. The attraction of empire wasn't merely economic, it was psychological. By the beginning of the twentieth century many people, and especially those proto-feminists collectively described as 'the New Women', felt circumscribed and stifled by this island, its rigid class and gender divisions, its openly professed philistinism and pragmatism. The island self-image was more than a geographical fact; it had become a mental straitjacket. Boys had always been encouraged to look for adventures, for freedom abroad. Now girls began to want these too, and not just as married appendages of a military or colonial administration, but in their own right. 'She was a strong and active woman, with long limbs and well-knit muscles, a clever fencer, a tireless swimmer, a fine horsewoman. But tonight she felt almost neurotic, like one of the weak or dissipated sisterhood for whom "rest cures" are invented.'

Domini has brains and passion as well as her boyish beauty.

Pre-Freud, Hichens has given her the family background to explain her nature: a religious mother who nevertheless runs off with her lover, abandoning her child and her husband, who becomes an embittered atheist. Domini finds her soulmate in the intense and brooding Androvsky, whom she marries and whose child she has, but when she discovers that he is a runaway monk she sends him back to the monastery, vowing herself to eternal chastity like his. Significantly, however, she doesn't return to England but stays on in Africa, in the Garden of Allah.

The form of the narrative allows the reader passion and physical freedom, but in saying that these must be paid for by ultimate renunciation, it assuages the guilt that such indulgence would otherwise bring. The exotic backdrop is part of the mechanism for setting the emotions free. Again like Corelli, Hichens manages to let the readers have their moral cake and eat it too. In the history of both publishing and society, such manifestations of popular culture, the soap operas of their day, are worth studying because of the insight they give into both temporary and more lasting needs of the human psyche. *The Garden of Allah* is a late Victorian phenomenon, but it also embodies material which can be found in Celtic and other mythology, and in medieval romance: the sexual, spiritual journey through another country, which frees the psychic traveller, if only for a time, from the taboos of custom and religion.

The desire to escape appears so often in different forms in Methuen's and other publishers' lists about this time that it must reflect some need in British society. It appears in the passionate adoption of the motor car into literature, both in motoring manuals and in fiction, particularly the novels of a husband and wife team, C. N. and A. M. Williamson, *The Lightning Conductor* and *The Princess Passes*. The manual *The Complete Motorist* is described in the Methuen Bulletin as 'a book which is technical but not repulsive', while the Williamsons' works are labelled 'a romance of the automobile and the open air' and 'The Romance of a Motor Car'. For children there was even a rewrite of *Struwelpeter* as *Petrol Peter*, an illustrated collection of cautionary motoring tales in verse.

For those who couldn't afford a car there was the bicycle, and for many readers who perhaps would never be able to leave England, there were travel books and the Little Guides which covered places of interest at home and abroad and were meant, I believe, to be both substitutes for travel as well as aids to it.

Escape can, of course, be in time as well as in space. History and especially the historical novel were, and still are, both vehicles for freeing the reader from the confines of everyday life and ways of allowing us to consider other possibilities and moralities. This yearning of the period finds its apotheosis in

*The History of Mr Polly*, a book which Methuen didn't publish for H. G. Wells, but which should be mentioned because it puts into contemporary lower-middle-class English dress, without the exotic disguise of other times or lands, the same fundamental desire for greater freedom, in Mr Polly's case, to begin all over again without the trammels of inadequacy and failure, the fetters of church, state and custom.

In Henry James's *The Golden Bowl*, which Methuen published in 1905, the distancing factor is wealth and position that allow James to consider the quasi-incestuous love between father and daughter which drives father to marry his new son-in-law's old mistress to keep her from harming his daughter. Algernon Methuen's continuing belief in James, in spite of poor sales, had been remarked by several members of the firm. *The Golden Bowl* was to be his reward, for it soon went into a second and third edition.

> The publication of a new book by Mr Henry James is a great literary event, and Mr James is one of the very few men of whom this statement can be made. It cannot indeed be said that he is the darling of the multitude but he is what he prefers to be – the giver of untold pleasure to the lover of style and of a profound psychological analysis.

Clearly Methuen knew what he was getting.

His defence of Oscar Wilde is equally firm in the announcement of the firm's intention to publish *De Profundis*, which Methuen had acquired from Robert Ross, Wilde's literary executor, in one octavo and two limited editions to test the water: 'fifty copies on Japanese paper and two hundred on large hand-made paper'. The book 'should take an enduring place in the literature of misfortune' and 'written in prison, expressed with unfailing lucidity the philosophy which he gathered in his two years' imprisonment, and is of great interest not only for the light it throws on the curiously complex nature of its author but also for its intrinsic beauty'.

This bold act obviously required considerable justification on Methuen's part for there is more apologia further on in the bulletin. 'The time has now passed when the public need fear the contagion of such a name, and *De Profundis* will rehabilitate the name of the author in the minds of those to whom the books of a man are of more importance than his private character.' The gamble was justified. Two months later Methuen was able to announce a third edition and to reprint at length rave reviews from the *Daily Mail*, *Daily News*, the *Star* the *St James Gazette* and *Westminster Gazette*, along with a page-length quote from the book itself.

Smithers had been Wilde's publisher in the last years of his life and brought out the immensely successful *Ballad of Reading*

*Gaol* in 1898. Among Methuen authors Wilde had numbered many friends, like Dowson, Frank Harris and Maeterlinck and some who, like W. E. Henley, had become enemies. John Lane, who had been Wilde's publisher before his imprisonment, had clearly no wish to renew the connection after his death. At first sight Methuen, the ex-schoolmaster, seems an unlikely figure to take it over, but this is exactly what he did, going on to reissue, under Robert Ross's editorship, the complete works in the next few years. Perhaps it was Ross himself who wanted to restore respectability at least to the work which publication by Smithers, whose reputation was that of a near pornographer, wouldn't have done. Unfortunately E. V. Lucas didn't see fit to republish that part of his correspondence with Ross that actually related to Wilde's work. Although the decision to publish must have been Methuen's, E. V. Lucas was the editor, claiming that he was responsible not only for the first abridgement but also for the title *De Profundis* in his *Reading, Writing and Remembering*: ' . . . it was I who was asked by Ross to prepare the printed version from Wilde's very disorderly draft. The title was mine and, rightly or wrongly I left out a great deal.'

He was also to leave out two or three of Wilde's letters, that Ross had shown in typescript, from an anthology in which he had wanted to include them. Lady Colvin, on hearing of this project, told Lucas that if Wilde's went in, then R. L. Stevenson's letters to her husband and herself would be out, so strong still was the feeling attached by some people to Wilde's name, which makes Methuen's decision to publish all the braver. Colvin, Lucas says, had the same passion for Stevenson (whose *Vailima Letters* to him had been one of Methuen's most successful early publications) as Ross had for Wilde. In 1914 he called 'Oscar Wilde-ism . . . the most pestilent and hateful disease our time'. Such considerations would not prevent Methuen from including both Stevenson and Wilde in his own *Anthology of Modern Verse* in 1921.

This anthology is, I think, more than just the schoolmaster again perceiving the need for a book and for fulfilling it. It reflects, as does the fine art list, Methuen's own very real interest in poetry. Many of the poets in it appear on the Methuen list in the years before the Great War, either as editors or writers. It was, after all, poetry which had given Methuen his first runaway success, and in 1908 there was a new edition of Kipling's poems uniform with Macmillan's edition of the prose. Kipling is of course in the 1921 anthology, which is still an excellent quick guide to that poetic period which the introduction by Robert Lynd labels 'Georgian' and 'modern', two epithets which now seem contradictory, though many critics would still agree with Methuen in his dedication 'To Thomas Hardy, greatest of the moderns.' Among the Methuen authors were H. C. Beeching, Laurence Binyon, W. H. Davies, Rose Fyleman, Kipling, Masefield, Quiller-Couch, Herbert Trench,

Francis Thomson, Wilde, Iolo Williams and Yeats. Two whose other work Methuen published before the Great War (though not for their poems) were Hilaire Belloc and G. K. Chesterton. E. J. Taylor remembers Belloc 'handsome, declaiming' as a frequent visitor to the Essex Street office, and Chesterton, who came rarely, as 'weighty and chuckling'. Other pre-War Methuen authors, though not for their poetry, were Ford Madox Hueffer, Ernest Dowson and, from the post-War period, the young T. S. Eliot and D. H. Lawrence.

# EMMANUEL BURDEN

### MERCHANT

OF THAMES ST., IN THE CITY OF
LONDON, EXPORTER OF HARDWARE

A RECORD OF
HIS LINEAGE, SPECULATIONS
LAST DAYS AND DEATH

BY

### HILAIRE BELLOC

WITH THIRTY-FOUR ILLUSTRATIONS
BY G. K. CHESTERTON

METHUEN & CO.
36 ESSEX STREET W.C.
LONDON

A SKETCH OF MR. BURDEN - FROM MEMORY

The Catholic group is particularly strong, both in the 1921 anthology and in the pre-War Methuen list, and included several converts like Maurice Baring, Dowson and Chesterton, as well as those born into the faith like Belloc. The wave of conversion continued after Cardinal Newman's death in 1890. Wilde himself had been received into the church on his death-bed but his leaning was, like Dowson's, towards an aesthetic version of Catholicism rather than the hearty medievalism of Old England which the 'Chesterbelloc' (as Shaw was to dub them) propagated in essays, poems, novels and even guide-books. Chesterton first appears in the Methuen list in 1906 with his biography of Dickens; Belloc was an old hand by then with *Emmanuel Burden, Merchant*; *Paris*; *Hills and the Sea*; *On Nothing* and *The Pyrenees*.

If it was hard for Frank Swinnerton in *The Georgian Literary Scene* of 1935 to assess Belloc and Chesterton's contribution to twentieth-century English literature, a further fifty years has made it no easier. Perhaps their work too should be seen as a manifestation of the period's desire to escape not only from the problems and mores of their time but also from the pressures increasingly exerted by science and technology, by reiterating Newman's view that the real universe isn't logical.

Two books which Methuen published in 1906, *Development and Divine Purpose* and *Religion in Evolution*, embody the scientific discoveries which were giving rise to doubt and the writer's attempts to reconcile Christianity and evolution. The firm's heaviest gun was Sir Oliver Lodge, the physicist and Christian apologist, whose *The Substance of Faith* and *Man and the Universe* Methuen published in 1907 and 1908. Although an Anglican, Methuen was liberal enough to allow the Catholic view an airing, especially when expressed with such frequency and with a fluency that had great popular appeal. Belloc's first novel, *Emmanuel Burden, Merchant* was published in 1904 with thirty-six illustrations by Chesterton. It's likely that Methuen and Belloc were long-standing political if not personal allies, since Belloc was elected Liberal MP for Salford in 1906. Methuen himself stood for Guildford as a Liberal in 1910, but failed to be elected. In 1905 he published *England's Ruin*, a pamphlet in favour of free trade and against his previous leader Joseph Chamberlain. Like Methuen, both Belloc and Chesterton were vociferously against the Boer War. Methuen re-published his own views on the subject in *The Tragedy of South Africa* in 1905.

Algernon Methuen suffered a mysterious but serious illness in 1907. The following year a book was published which, like Kipling's *Barrack-Room Ballads*, was ultimately to be a runaway bestseller for many years. The Methuen announcements ran:

> No popular writer has given his admirers so little as the author of *The Golden Age* and *Dream Days* – both classics already. It is several years since the latter was published, and now at last Mr Grahame breaks his long silence with *The Wind in the Willows*, a fantastic and whimsical satire upon life – or allegory of life – the author's amusing device being to show the reader the real thing as if it were the play of small woodland and riverside creatures.

Several reviewers suggested that the book needed illustrating to be a real success, but it succeeded without and was already a classic by the time Paul Bronson produced the first complete set of illustrations in 1913. Patrick Chalmers, whose *Kenneth Grahame: Life, Letters and Unpublished Work* Methuen published

in 1933, a year after Grahame's death, gives no indication of how the book first came to Methuen instead of to John Lane, who had already published Grahame's *The Golden Age* and *Dream Days* with great success. Originally called *The Wind in the Reeds*, and indeed first advertised as such, the book had begun as bedtime stories for, and letters to, Grahame's small son Alastair, known as 'Mouse'. The manuscript was written down when the Grahames moved to Cookham Dene and Kenneth left the Bank of England after an attack of influenza.

Kenneth Grahame's letter to his son Alastair, with the tale of a toad

16, Durham Villas, Campden Hill. W.

21 June 1907.

My dearest Mouse

No doubt you will be interested to hear the further adventures of M^r Toad, after he gallopped away across country on the bargee's horse, with the bargee shouting after him in vain. Well presently the horse got tired of galloping so fast, and broke from a gallop into a trot, and then from a trot into a walk, & then he stopped altogether & began to nibble grass. And the toad looked round about him & found he was on a large common. On the common stood a gipsy tent, and a gipsy man was sitting beside it, on a bucket turned upside down, smoking. In front of the tent a fire of sticks was burning, & over the fire hung an iron pot, and out of the pot came steam, & bubblings, and the most beautiful good smell that ever you smelt.

It was first shown to the American magazine *Everybody's*, but they rejected it. The change in title was occasioned by the similarity of the first version, *The Wind in the Reeds*, to the title of a volume of poems by W. B. Yeats. Graham Robertson, a close friend of Grahame's who was to produce the first frontispiece, made several suggestions for alternative titles, but it isn't clear from Chalmers's account who was finally responsible for what was to become such a famous name. By 1909, however lukewarm some of the reviewers had been, the book already numbered Theodore Roosevelt and Arthur Deakin, the Prime Minister of Australia, among its steadily growing body of fans. By 1909 it was in its fourth edition, but Methuen editions could be quite small; by 1911 it had notched up one more, and by 1913 it had reached the eighth, still with its one frontispiece by Robertson.

Someone who was to rival Kenneth Grahame for many years as a top Methuen children's author first appeared in the list in 1910, A. A. Milne with *The Day's Play*. The advertisement for the collection read: 'The name of A. A. Milne may not yet have come into the ken of the general reader but the initials A. A. M. surely have, for it is thus that he has for some three years past signed his weekly fantasy in *Punch*, to whose round table he is the latest recruit.' In fact Milne was assistant editor of *Punch* under Sir Owen Seaman from 1906 to 1914. Methuen was to continue to publish his early collections, both prose and verse, of *Punch* contributions, followed by his plays, like the very successful *Mr Pim Passes By*, after the Great War, without, of course, being able to foresee that Milne would become one of the most famous writers on Methuen's or any other children's list. In return, Milne was to remain loyal to the firm for the rest of his enormously varied and prolific writing life, even though he was to come to feel that his four children's books had destroyed his reputation as a serious writer. 'It is easier in England,' he wrote in 1938 when his last play was a failure, 'to make a reputation than to lose one.'

E. V. Lucas had been invited to join the *Punch* round table in 1904, succeeding Phil May, whose album Methuen had already published, and presumably Lucas was the firm's link with Milne. Lucas was already the British representative of Harper and Co., the American publisher. In his capacity as reader, which he was rather inclined to play down in later years, he was paid £800 a year as a talent scout by Methuen and was very soon made a director after the business became a private company in 1910.

It's not clear why Methuen should have taken this step of making the firm a private company when he did. Perhaps he thought that the size and turnover of the firm warranted it at last. From the beginning Lucas was both director and shareholder. The other two directors were Algernon Methuen himself as chairman and George Webster as managing director.

LADY MARY WORTLEY MONTAGU
(Enamel)
By John Stephen Liotard (?)

# MINIATURES
## ANCIENT AND MODERN

BY

CYRIL DAVENPORT

AUTHOR OF "JEWELLERY," ETC.

WITH A FRONTISPIECE IN COLOUR
AND FORTY-FIVE OTHER ILLUSTRATIONS

METHUEN & CO.
36 ESSEX STREET W.C.
LONDON

OLD · KING · COLE · WAS · A ·
MERRY · OLD · SOUL ·

# A BOOK · OF NURSERY · RHYMES

ILLUSTRATED · BY · FRANCIS · D · BEDFORD
PUBLISHED · BY · METHUEN · & · Cº
36 · ESSEX · STREET
STRAND · W · C ·

Frederick Muller, who variously looked after education and illustration, became company secretary. Almost at once, Methuen offered some of his own shares to members of staff and by 1912 nineteen of them had taken up the offer and attended the annual general meeting. Spencer Killby, the production manager, and C. W. Chamberlain, head of the trade department, were added to the board in 1912. Instead of Christmas bonuses the shareholding staff were paid dividends.

The effect of all this was to emphasise and encourage staff loyalty, always an important question for Methuen himself, who made a point of mentioning it in his AGM speeches. Nevertheless, there were defections, notably in 1908 of G. R. Mills and Charles Boon to found the firm of that name. Many of the staff were recruited from the same Church of England secondary school, St Augustine's in Kilburn, except for Killby who, like Chamberlain, had come via Kegan Paul. This also helped to maintain staff loyalty in the face of what seems to have been George Webster's rather abrasive management, to which Algernon Methuen himself had to provide a more affable counterpoise.

Methuen made clear in a speech at an early annual general meeting that he was working on the principle of pushing the shilling and sevenpenny books, mostly novels, as the bread-and-butter line. By 1911 there were nearly 170 authors on the fiction list, many of them with several titles. Of these, some seventy were women and a hundred men. Those whose names are still recognisable three-quarters of a century later include W. W. Jacobs, Hilaire Belloc, Arnold Bennett, Joseph Conrad, Arthur Conan Doyle, George Gissing, Ford Madox Hueffer (Ford), Henry James, Jack London, Lucas himself, A. E. W. Mason, A. A. Milne, E. F. Benson, H. G. Wells, Maurice Baring and Somerville and Ross. Two at least have had books made into television series.

These weren't, however, bestselling authors, apart from Arnold Bennett, who was just entering this class with *Clayhanger*, and the immensely popular W. W. Jacobs. The bestselling authors form, on the whole, a separate list still headed by Corelli but now closely followed by Anthony Hope; Robert Hichens; E. Maria Albanesi; Bernard Capes; B. M. Croker; the daughter of Charles Kingsley, Lucas Malet; Mrs M. E. Mann; John Oxenham; Gilbert Parker; Eden Philpotts; W. Pett Ridge; H. B. Marriot Watson; the Williamsons with their motoring novels; F. W. Bain with his Indian stories, and, still reprinting, Sabine Baring-Gould. These all had several titles in print which ran to many editions. Often their books were appearing simultaneously at six shillings, two shillings and sixpence, one shilling, sevenpence and in the monthly sixpenny *Novelist*. There was still at this period no real rival to the novel for leisure pastime, and women in particular, who were much more restricted in their activities than men, read avidly. The only truly popular alternatives to fiction were the theatre and the music hall.

How much popular fiction contributed to or retarded women's suffrage is an interesting question. In 1907 Methuen published Elizabeth Robins's *The Convert*, which is a well-written piece of propaganda from a writer who had already had a suffrage play called *Votes for Women* performed at the Royal Court, then simply The Court Theatre. From the number of known suffragette writers whom he published, including the cousins Somerville and Ross whose *Dan Russell, the Fox* appeared in 1911, it would seem as if Algernon Methuen's Liberalism included votes for women, in spite of the marked lack of support for women's suffrage from Marie Corelli, whose views must reflect the ambiguous or negative attitudes of many of her readers.

*Crown 8vo, 6s.*

# THE CONVERT

BY

## ELIZABETH ROBINS

THIS is an important new novel by Elizabeth Robins, the author of "The Magnetic North." Miss Robins, who is a passionate believer in the power of women, and who is the author of the recent successful play at the Court Theatre, is giving her forthcoming story a strong feminine interest, and it will be found to be one of the frankest and most moving expositions of the limitations amidst which the sex, especially single women, have to exist that has yet been written. This will be Miss Robins' first romance since her wonderfully successful book "The Magnetic North."

METHUEN & CO.
36 ESSEX STREET W.C.
LONDON

[P.T.O.

Advertisement for Elizabeth Robins's *The Convert* (1907)

Conrad himself is an interesting case. In *Under Western Eyes* his narrator uses the term 'feminist' to describe the deeply unattractive and corrupt revolutionary Peter Ivanovitch. Yet at the same time the heroine is another of those boyish athletic girls full of intelligence and independence, and a practical revolutionary who returns to Russia to work among the poor and imprisoned. He had written to 'Jack' Galsworthy about the book as early as 1908, expressing his hopes for its financial as

well as artistic success. He had been doing his accounts and for eleven novels reckoned he had averaged £650 a year.

Published in 1912, *Under Western Eyes* is one of the very few books on the list to suggest that Europe and the larger world were sliding towards chaos, though its setting is pre-revolutionary Russia and its characters belong to anarchist and liberal factions, rather than foreshadowing the European conflict which was only two years away. Perhaps Methuen himself didn't want to believe it for, in the same year, he published the only explicit contribution to what must have been occupying at least some people's minds, in Colonel H. B. Hanna's *Can Germany Invade England?*, which proved to the author's and no doubt many readers' satisfaction that she couldn't, or at least not with any hope of success as long as there was a Royal Navy. The quotation from von Schellendorff on the paper cover, suggesting that the German Navy would need complete command of the sea before an invasion, sounds uncomfortably like Goering's plans for complete control of the air before Operation 'Sea-lion' a generation later.

Even though it was 1912, Hanna was still questioning the Entente Cordiale and refusing to see Germany as the enemy, regarding her instead as a 'great nation'. His attitude reflects the general upreparedness for war, which was so widespread that the Conrads were marooned in Poland at the outbreak of war. They had gone to recuperate on the proceeds of *Chance*, whose success had brought at least the offer of £1,000 for magazine serialisation and £850, presumably from Methuen, for volume rights in Conrad's next book, as he wrote in delight to Galsworthy in May 1914.

Endpapers from F. G. Brabant's *Sussex* (1900)

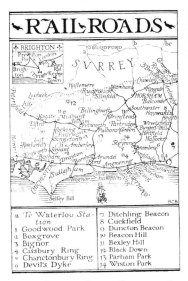

Such mentions of money in writers' letters to each other are quite rare, as indeed are mentions of publishers at all. However, to open a volume of letters from one of the Methuen list is to find the others constantly addressed or spoken of: Wells to Gissing, Bennett to Wells, Conrad to Galsworthy and everyone to and from Hueffer. Gissing in 1898 wrote to Wells that his then agent W. M. Colles had got him an *advance* (his italics) of £250 from Methuen for *The Town Traveller*, which his new agent (J. B. Pinker, who was also agent for Conrad, and eventually for Bennett, who had been with Colles too) had increased to £300 for *The Crown of Life* in 1899. If there was rivalry between them all it didn't stop them from trying to help each other to publication, as Conrad did in recommending Norman Douglas to E. V. Lucas, who passed his manuscript to Algernon Methuen, always the final judge. He offered, after what seemed to the anxious Conrad a lengthy wait, a cooperative publishing deal which Conrad knew Douglas couldn't afford, and that must have been one of the old-style agreements, recorded in the 1890s accounts, and of which perhaps the most famous and important was to be Ronald Firbank's agreement with Grant Richards for the publication of his novels.

H. M. Batson's *A Book of the Country and the Garden* (1903)

their own in an ignoble place under some standards, and failing sadly still. Spenser, also, in which I indulged freely without any experience to guide me, turned out to be scentless, and though in most years an admirable doer, it is consequently devoid of charm for me. It is a sport from Baroness Rothschild, or from her progeny Her Majesty, and inherits this bad quality from her.

EATS ALL THE BLOOMS HE CAN REACH

*July 15.* Crimson Rambler over a bower is looking exquisite. It ought to be grown with The Garland, if any combination is desired with it. The two bloom together, and the white and crimson look well intermixed. An old-fashioned eve green rose, Flora, on a north wall is good in many useful respects. It makes rampant wood, and one can cut great boughs of it for the house. Its shell-tinted little blossoms are beautiful of their kind, though they would not satisfy those persons

who must have all their flowers of the largest size. A hedge of white Ayrshires and pink hedge-roses has been spoilt by the new pony, who puts his head over and eats all the blooms he can reach, with not a few thorns as well.

EVENING PRIMROSES IN THE WILD GARDEN

The yellow alströmerias are in full glory. There is a round bed of them, edged with *funkia grandiflora*, whose beautiful fringe leads the long stems of the alströmerias gently into the ground. Many persons refrain from growing alströmerias because they do not consider them hardy, but they are hardy enough if planted nine inches below the surface, and unis hollow. It is a seed-vessel, and is filled with seeds. The seeds cannot grow without pollen. If pollen gets on the stigma, the sticky stigma holds it fast. The pollen finds its way down

*Nectar-Guide (one of the five pink lines that act as nectar-guides)*

Convolvulus, showing Bee entering Flower for Honey

through the long stem to the little seeds. It nourishes them, and they grow. But if the pollen does not come, the seeds die.

A flower's own pollen does not usually make the finest seed. The small green bodies in the

seed-vessel usually ripen faster and produce the best seed when the stigma has received pollen from another flower of the same kind. Sometimes, even, a flower's own pollen is no more use to it than so much sand.

Now we, while visiting the flowers for nectar, get our furry coats dusted with pollen, and carry it from blossom to blossom. This is why the flowers make nectar. They do it to coax the bees to come.

*Tongue thrust into Nectary*

Diagram showing Bee extracting Honey from Convolvulus

Now watch me enter this pretty convolvulus flower; here is a line to act as nectar-guide, leading to the nectar-cups, five of them filled to the brim with sweet, clear nectar. Perhaps you wonder how I can get my head into the tiny openings that lead to the nectar. Look, and you will soon find out.

Ah! now you see my long shining brown tongue, and you notice how strong and flexible

M. W. Morley's *The Bee People* (1907)

Many of the writers lived in Sussex at least for part of their lives, feeling no need, as writers have come to do, to keep in such close touch with London. There were, after all, frequent trains and the post. Algernon Methuen himself seems increasingly after his illness in 1907 to have stayed in Surrey, coming up once a week but keeping in constant touch by post and the new device of the telephone. Aside from the firm, his passion, which he shared with his wife, was still the garden and in particular the cultivation of alpine plants, on which he wrote and published a little book.

Others may have resented this absorbing hobby and felt it caused him to pay less attention to the company, though not, on the whole, his employees, who knew the meticulous attention he gave to every detail. Arnold Bennett was certainly resentful, attempting on one occasion at least to inspire rebellion in E. V. Lucas, who was trying to put together the ill-fated Methuen Annual in 1914. Bennett wrote to Pinker his agent:

> As regards the *Methuen Annual*, I have received a request from Lucas; I may tell you that I talked to him straight. I pointed out to him that the astute Methuen was simply using him as a tool, and that I had no intention whatever

48

of allowing Methuen to walk up and down his gardens chuckling over the idea that he had been clever enough to rope in the golden calves at a smaller expenditure than other people....

The half-joking but fundamentally tetchy tone is typical of Bennett and his relations with the firm. Unlike Conrad, whose work he had always admired, Algernon Methuen hadn't solicited Bennett, even when he knew that Bennett was already fretful on the Chatto list in 1900. On that occasion Bennett wrote to his first agent Colles: 'What a self convicted and ingrained nincompoop Methuen is! How blind to the dazzling success that awaits him. However he has been advising Philpotts to imitate *Cranford* and a man who would do that would also do anything short of marry Marie Corelli.' By 1903, however, when he had moved at Wells's instigation to J. B. Pinker, he wrote in a modified tone to him from Paris: 'With regard to Methuen I do not personally see how we can do anything with him, at any rate at present. And I don't think he can sell more copies of a book than Chatto.... The only drawback of Chatto is that my serious books seem always rather lonely and peculiar in his lists....'

Two years later the tone has changed. Writing again to Pinker he says: 'What I want is to be published by Methuen. How soon can I get there? Chatto's list gives me appendicitis....' Methuen himself, however, was being coy and Bennett was still writing to his agent in 1907: 'I quite agree that if Methuen is not keen Methuen is not our man....'

Methuen's difficulty was that fundamentally he thought Bennett's work might be seen as, or even actually be, too hasty and therefore slapdash. Methuen understood the agonies and slowness of Conrad. With Bennett he wanted no more than a book a year. Bennett of course rejected any suggestion of deficiency in his work. Again to Pinker in 1909, when they were not in active negotiation to move to Methuen, he writes:

> I shall be glad if Methuen or another competent critic, Lucas for instance, will examine any of this work, and say if it bears any signs of haste or slovenliness.... Two months is my time for an ordinary novel. I know I am singular. But it is me Methuen has to deal with.... As for my work being taken seriously we shall see about that.... He had the chance of having me eight years ago and refused it.

They agreed finally and Bennett was able to write in February 1910: 'I have finished the first part of the Methuen novel. It will be called *Clayhanger*. The whole thing will be finished on June 30th. I shall not have the second novel of the trilogy ready for publication before autumn 1911. Perhaps this news will

(*opposite clockwise*)
Arnold Bennet

E. V. Lucas

Kenneth Grahame

Hilaire Belloc

A BOOKSELLERS'

XV

WHAT *was* a Publisher?
   A Crœsus whom,
Meek authors, wavering 'twixt
   Hope and Gloom,
Clasping their Rags about
   their shivering Forms,
Waited and fawned on in his
   sumptuous Room.

XVI

WHAT *is* a Publisher? A
   Craven whom,
Sitting dejected, conscious of
   his Doom,
With Ruin at his Elbow
   Night and Day,
Sleek Agents bully in his
   squalid Room.
   [ 10 ]

RUBÁIYÁT

XVII

WHAT is a Bookseller?
   Too many Firms
Are represented here; the Poet
   squirms
From naked Truth; but let
   it go at this:
One whose controlling Hope is
   Better Terms

XVIII

NO Harm in that: 'tis
   Human Nature tells.
But here's the Joke which
   Gravity dispels:
That every Bookseller the
   wide World through
Wants Better Terms than Any-
   body else.
   [ 11 ]

comfort Methuen. . . .' He was to be paid £300, £350 and £400 for the next three books.

An example of E. V. Lucas's ready wit

Arthur Waugh at Chatto was annoyed with Pinker at Bennett's defection and, not knowing how long the thing had been brewing, thought that they had acted hastily in going over to Methuen. He might, however, on reflection have been glad to have escaped the problems of Bennett's temperament. To set him beside Conrad's doubts and scrupulous crafts-manship is to see both ends of the author spectrum.

> I particularly want you to take the line with Methuen that he must expect all sorts of different things from me and plenty of them; and that it should be his business to make the best of them. The question is not whether my method of producing is the best way commercially and artistically – it is the only way I have of producing. It is not the slightest use any publisher trying to cork me up. . . . I never rewrote any portion of any book. My first draft is always the final writing. . . .

The relationship continued to be uneasy. Methuen was always quick to write and tell Bennett how much he liked a new book. In his turn Bennett was adamant in his own interest, whether it was in the matter of the jacket for *These Twain* in 1915, 'the horrible ugliness of the whole thing – colouring and drawing – As regards the woman the blouse is incredible,' or the right to regain his books for the cheap editions, without the fifty-pound recompense demanded, when Methuen withdrew from the sixpenny novel market in 1913.

By 1922 he was complaining that Methuen's not being in the business of buying serial rights put them at a disadvantage.

Methuen wrote saying how much he admired *Mr Prohack* and hoped Bennett wasn't going to desert them. Once in 1914 they were joined at the Reform by Henry James, who said that for him it was now a club of ghosts.

It was at the Reform too that over lunch in 1916 Methuen told Bennett and Pinker about the 'revolution' in the price of novels suggested by the Publishers Association council 'on which only four members published novels on any scale,' Bennett wrote in his journal: 'Characteristic. We told him that the scheme of different prices would never work, and coached him as to what he should say at the grand meeting on Monday.'

By then the world was at war. The last pre-war annual general meeting of the company in 1913 had heard 'that business had not been quite as good as was hoped but still profits were quite satisfactory. There were rivals in the field so far as cheap books were concerned, and it would be necessary more than ever before to pursue the business with energy.' The three salaried directors were Methuen himself and the managing director, George Webster, both on £1,200 a year, and E. V. Lucas, at that time earning £600. Much of the company's money was wisely invested in a variety of stock, from railways to government bonds. The usual dividend was $2\frac{1}{2}\%$ three times a year. In 1913 the company had a turnover from sales of £107,000. Four years later this had risen to £145,000. In between there was a war to be got through.

The programme and menu for the staff river outing in June 1914

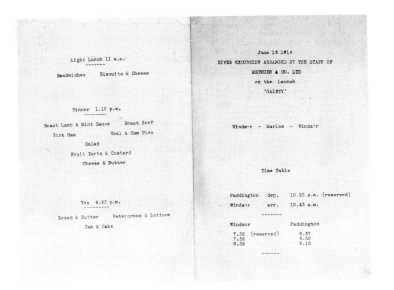

# SWOLLEN-HEADED
# WILLIAM

Painful Stories and Funny Pictures
After the German!

Text adapted by E. V. Lucas

Drawings adapted by Geo. Morrow

LONDON
METHUEN & CO., LTD.

# THREE

# *Dulce et Decorum*
## 1914–1918

Joseph Conrad and his wife were not the only ones caught
out by the suddenness of the war. Young Taylor of the trade
department, on holiday in Switzerland at the end of July, was
worried only about the possibility of a choppy crossing and had
no idea that war was about to break out. Nothing in the
spring list of announcements had prepared him for the 'Great
Struggle', as the autumn catalogue described it. Indeed, Frank
Swinnerton, who was published by Methuen at this time,
alleges that Algernon suggested to younger writers that they
should suspend work for the duration, presumably expecting
it to be short, and to the more established that they should take
a 50 per cent cut in advances. As a devoted member of the
Liberal Party, Algernon Methuen secured the rights to both the
Prime Minister's speeches in a series of pamphlets, and the
King's message to his people. The company swung into top
gear behind the war effort and, divining at once that in wartime
people turn to poetry, reissued Kipling with a special edition
of 'Recessional' on an illuminated hanging card. E. V. Lucas
rewrote *Struwelpeter* yet again as *Swollen-Headed William*, a
send-up of the Kaiser and what the British saw as the Prussian
mentality, and there was a section called 'Sea, Air, Land' on
different aspects of the armed forces.

Kipling's wasn't the only verse. Behind or below any great
achievement in a literary field lies the seedbed of activity, a
hidden two-thirds of intense fermentation which throws up the
peaks. If the recognised eminences among the poets of the Great
War are Owen, Sassoon, Brooke and Thomas, below or around
them were a cluster of other writers. Methuen's list can have
been no exception. Suddenly the amount of poetry doubled,
with Alfred Noyes, a reprint of Bret Harte, W. H. Davies, Maeterlinck and John Oxenham all published in the first six months
of the war. The titles are an immediate indication of their stance
and contents. From Alfred Noyes came *The White Cliffs*, *The
Searchlights* and *A Salute from the Fleet*. Bret Harte's reprint was
*The Reveille* and Oxenham produced a *Hymn For the Men at the
Front*.

There were other offerings: G. K. Chesterton wrote *Letters to
an Old Garibaldean*, pointing out that Italy belonged with Britain

and France; Anthony Hope produced the *New German Testament*; and A. C. Clutton-Brock, one of a line of popular soothsayers which in our own time has included Kingsley Martin and Malcolm Muggeridge, uttered his first volume of *Thoughts on the War*.

Like many other people, Algernon Methuen had expected in 1914 that the war would be quite short; nevertheless, he took the precaution of ordering enough paper for 50,000 novels and as the AGM minutes for 1915 noted, this prudence ensured that the company suffered no great deprivation of paper stocks, although prices rose inexorably. The young men of all departments began to enlist at once, creating another shortage, that of manpower, which was relieved in its turn by the appointment of the first women workers in the office, some of whom were quick to join in Methuen's shareholding scheme and to take their places at the AGM.

The military tone even crept into the minutes of the first wartime AGM on 19 December when:

> the Chairman said that we met in exceptional circumstances which were not likely to recur in our lifetime. He was glad to say that the reduction in trade was not so great as had been anticipated, and it had been possible to keep the flag flying. . . . Nine of our members had offered their services to the country and were now fulfilling their duty in various ways, and he thought he would be expressing the feelings of those present if he sent them our very best wishes and hopes that they would all return safe and sound and with glorious memories . . . he hardly thought we could keep up the standard of the last year or so, so far as profits were concerned.

Algernon Methuen was absent from the next year's meeting, when the managing director George Webster commented: 'little did we think at the last statutory meeting that the war would still be in progress', and went on to speak of 'difficulties in many directions'. After a little self-congratulation on having anticipated the limiting regulations on paper and noting that now twenty-one of the forty-seven staff were in the forces while four had attested, it was agreed to suggest a staff roll of honour to the absent chairman.

Though the business had been 'fair, profits [had] not been any better than forecast by Mr Methuen in 1914'. All of those present must have been aware of a 'difficulty' that was studiously not being minuted, even though the 1915 statutory meeting was being held late in March 1916, presumably because at the time when it should have been held in mid-December 1915, the firm was smarting under the deep wounds, legend has it, of the fires of the common hangman, who had just burnt a thousand copies of D. H. Lawrence's *The Rainbow* outside the Royal Exchange.

P. H. Ditchfield's *London Survivals* (1914)

Lawrence had first been published by Duckworth through the influence of Edward Garnett, but the company had lost about £16 on *Sons and Lovers* and weren't eager for more. The ubiquitous Pinker, perhaps at the instigation of Arnold Bennett, who greatly admired Lawrence's work, had stepped in to offer Lawrence a £300 advance from Methuen for his new book *The Rainbow*. Eager to get married to Frieda and, as usual at this time, desperate for money, Lawrence signed up both Pinker, whom he was later to call a 'little parvenu snob of a procurer of books', and Methuen. Even before he finished it, Lawrence felt that the book might cause his new publisher problems. ' ... when Methuen gets *The Rainbow*, he'll wonder what changeling is foisted on him. For it is different from my other work. I am glad with it. I am coming into my full feather at last, I think,' he wrote to A. W. McLeod in January.

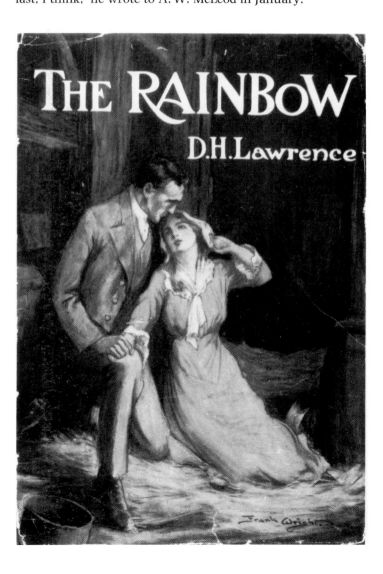

56

When someone in the firm actually got round to reading it, the manuscript was returned for extensive revisions as 'unpublishable as it stood'. Lawrence worked on these until the following March and the book was published on 30 September 1915. The reviews were extremely hostile, linking Lawrence's eroticism to the war by suggesting that such 'filth' was a betrayal of the men who were fighting and dying 'for liberty'. The firm had anticipated trouble and had written to Pinker three days before publication that they hoped Lawrence 'will try to modify his broadmindedness in the next novel'.

There must have been a certain amount of carelessness in checking that the changes had been carried out as Pinker had clearly assured the firm that they had. This seems unlike Algernon's usual meticulousless. Perhaps he himself was too preoccupied with the war, which had initially gone badly for Britain and her allies. Presumably, as was usually the case, the author had written most of the blurb himself, as he had been asked to do in March. It was a good list in which to appear. There was Wells's *Bealby*, Conrad's *Victory*, two books by Bennett, a new Anthony Hope, *Something New* by P. G. Wodehouse and *The Elixir of Life* by Arthur Ransome. Altogether twenty-three new novels were announced, several by stalwarts like W. Pett Ridge and G. A. Birmingham, and, significantly, another newcomer, at least to Methuen, Sax Rohmer. Lawrence is described, presumably not in this bit by himself, as 'one of the most remarkable of the younger school of novelists'. The story:

> contains a history of the Brangwen character through its developing crises of love, religion, and social passion, from the time when Tom Brangwen, the well-to-do Derbyshire farmer, marries a Polish lady, widow of an exile in England, to the moment when Ursula, his granddaughter, the leading shoot of the restless, fearless family, stands waiting at the advance post of our time to blaze a path into the future.

The future that Lawrence envisaged wasn't one that offered comfort to those countering the British losses in the Dardanelles with the jingoism of near-despair. Bennett had been to the front in France and Belgium and sent back his dispatches. There was inevitably some tub-thumping, but the devastation so close to Paris, still for English intellectuals the hub of the 'civilised world', had clearly shocked him, and his outrage is that of a frightened bourgeois trying to maintain his British phlegm. If Paris, why not London? *Can the Germans Invade England?* was suddenly more than a textbook enquiry. Nevertheless, Bennett was to be one of the few to protest against the treatment of *The Rainbow*.

Two reviews in particular seem to have brought the book to

someone's attention: I say someone because it is not impossible that a common informer lies somewhere behind the initial police move. James Douglas in the *Star* said of it that the book had 'no right to exist' and Clement Shorter in the *Sphere* wrote: 'There is no form of viciousness, of suggestiveness, that is not reflected in these pages.' Robert Lynd called it 'a monstrous wilderness of phallicism'. However, Douglas, who was to be much quoted in the trial, pinpointed an added cause of outrage in his closing words: 'The young men who are dying for liberty are moral beings. They are the living repudiation of such impious denials of life as *The Rainbow*. The life they lay down is a lofty thing. It is not the thing that creeps and crawls in the these pages.'

Detective Inspector Albert Draper of New Scotland Yard was sent with a search warrant to the Essex Street offices on 3 November to seize the offending copies. Algernon Methuen wasn't in the office. It was George Webster, and Frederick Muller, the company secretary, who received Detective Inspector Draper. Presumably Algernon was telephoned, if indeed he was in the country. According to Methuen's account of what happened, given to the Society of Authors on 16 November, they were then assured by 'solicitors', presumably representing the police, that because of the firm's reputation, if they agreed to the removal of the books, the premises needn't be searched. They hastened to agree, and as soon as Inspector Draper had left, Webster and Muller telephoned Pinker.

On 11 November, Inspector Draper called again with a summons requiring Methuen to show cause why the books should not be destroyed. They understood from him that this was 'merely a formal matter to obtain our consent to the destruction of the book' and that if they agreed, the case needn't be heard in a public court. Misled by this, they failed to obtain legal assistance or make arrangements to be legally represented. Algernon Methuen must have been deeply shocked, even though they had half expected trouble. The Director of Public Prosecutions, Sir Charles Matthews, had initiated proceedings on behalf of the Commissioner of Police. The solicitor for the prosecution was Herbert Muskett; the magistrate was Sir John Dickinson, whose son had been killed at the front six weeks before.

Meanwhile, the Lawrences had managed with the help of the Asquiths to get passports for America, and Lawrence had been down to Garsington drumming up support and money from Lady Ottoline Morrell, only coming up to London two days before the trial. History doesn't record what must have passed between him and the firm. It's impossible to believe that there wasn't some kind of meeting or at least a telephone call.

The case came before Dickinson at Bow Street Magistrates Court on Saturday 13 November, not, as they had been led to believe, in private but in open court. Methuen were summoned

to show cause why the 1,011 copies should not be destroyed. No defence was offered. Methuen expressed regret that the book should have been published. They laid the blame on a reader, the agent and the author, and got away with costs of ten guineas and the destruction of the copies, by playing up the changes they had asked for and had been assured of. A letter from D. H. Lawrence to Pinker about the changes as late as 26 July had said: 'I have cut out as I said I would all the *phrases* objected to. The passages and paragraphs marked I cannot alter.... Tell Methuen he need not be afraid ...' Perhaps the most astonishing, and in a way humiliating, claim made by the firm during the trial was that the homosexual chapter had been read by two members of the staff who had failed to understand what it was about. Muskett took the opportunity to warn booksellers that anyone who attempted to sell the book was also liable to prosecution and the examining magistrate expressed his satisfaction that the circulating libraries hadn't taken it. He went on to say that he had never read anything more disgusting and that it was 'utter filth'.

According to Methuen, they had asked Inspector Draper if the author should be consulted about the destruction of the books and he had replied that the police case was only against the publishers and the author had no right to appear in the matter. If Methuen had indeed taken legal advice, it might have been rather different.

Meanwhile Clive Bell had telephoned, presumably at Lawrence's instigation, saying that he wanted to write in defence of Lawrence and his work. Muller had hastily telephoned Pinker in his turn, urging that no such thing should be done and saying that the firm felt very strongly that the whole thing should be hushed up. The secretary of the Society of Authors had written to Lawrence before the trial on the 10 November saying that the suppression of his work had been brought to their attention by W. L. George, another Methuen author, and inviting him to become a member so that they could consider his case. He had promptly asked Philip Morrell to propose him and joined at once.

Philip Morrell, Ottoline's pacifist MP husband, who had made their home at Garsington not only a refuge for artists but for 'conchies', asked questions twice in the House of Commons, on 18 November and 1 December, presumably without the support of Algernon Methuen. Apparently the Home Secretary, Sir John Simon's answering brief was marked with a note in red ink referring to Frieda, now of course Mrs Lawrence: 'As to a Mrs Weekley living at an address of D. H. Lawrence, see 352857.' This neatly connects anti-patriotism with licentiousness, since she was German by birth and the cousin of Von Richthofen, the Red Baron.

Why did the publisher of *De Profundis* and republisher of all Wilde's works so completely lose his nerve? Lawrence wrote of

Sir Algernon getting into his car
at New Place

him much later in 1925 that Methuen 'almost wept before the
magistrate when he was summoned for bringing out a piece of
indecent literature. He said he did not know the dirty thing he
had been handling, his reader had misadvised him – and
Peccavi! Peccavi! wept the now beknighted gentleman.'
Immediately after the trial Lawrence called Methuen 'a skunk'
in a letter to Constance Garnett, saying that he had 'left the
book entirely in the lurch: whined and puked, said not a word
for it ...' Lawrence suggests that this was Methuen himself but
the *Daily Telegraph* merely mentioned 'a member of the firm'.
It seems unlikely that Algernon would have escaped so anony-
mously. There were, I think, several reasons for the publisher's
response. The first was undoubtedly Algernon Methuen's
involvement with the Liberal government of Asquith, a government soon to be replaced, after the catastrophes of 1915, by a
coalition. Perhaps he had already been promised the baronetcy
he was given in mid-1916. If so, this was likely to be put at
risk by the prosecution, especially if Methuen had attempted to
defend the publication of a book that was anti-war and pro-
sex. Even before the prosecution Lady Cynthia Asquith had
noted in her diary of 18 October that, dining with the Prime
Minister at Downing Street, she had been 'much chaffed about
D. H. Lawrence.... Apparently *The Rainbow* is causing an

60

explosion on account of its "belly" etc. motif.' This shows that it had attracted attention in government circles.

Algernon wasn't by nature a warmonger or a coward. He had opposed the Boer War publicly in print and he had not been afraid to disagree with Joseph Chamberlain, also in public. But he had rightly gauged that this was the wrong moment to uphold Lawrence, even though Bennett, at the height of his popularity, as well as others, would undoubtedly have supported him. In a letter to E. V. Lucas in January 1916 Bennett wrote: 'I regret to say that I wrote 272,000 words last year. Equal to the British casualties for six months. Shorter had the cheek to write and ask me for an autographed copy of one of my books the other day. I sent him *The Author's Craft*. He has not seen the joke.' Shorter of course had badly lashed *The Rainbow* in his review.

Bennett had sold 13,000 copies of *These Twain* in the first week, as he discovered from lunching with Algernon Methuen at the Reform Club in January 1916. He, too, was complaining of 'some rotten reviews. Apart from other things the book is too jolly true for some people.' He obviously identified strongly with Lawrence in his treatment but it doesn't seem as though he was at this stage blaming the firm.

The Society of Authors had written both to the firm and to Pinker for their views on the case, and knowing that they were taking an interest, the Lawrences postponed their plans to sail to America. Pinker said that Lawrence had done all the revisions Methuen had asked for except for one paragraph, thus justifying to some extent Methuen's defence that the author had refused to alter any more. On 18 November the secretary at the Society of Authors wrote to Philip Morrell sending him some cuttings which were presumably newspaper accounts of the trial and asking in return for a report of the response to his first question in the House of Commons.

The secretary, Herbert Thring, had also written to R. C. Carton, who usually dealt with League of Dramatists' matters, requesting his opinion of *The Rainbow*. The answer came back on the 21st. Carton thought that there was 'nothing much more exceptionable in the book than in the work of G. E. Moore' except for the very explicit delineation of the erotic relationship between two women which was unusual. 'If censorship is to exist at all the above episode would almost seem to invite prohibition from the English Market.'

Thring wrote back the next day: ' ... Thank you for your little note on *The Rainbow*. I certainly won't let it get into print. I only wanted your opinion and it will save me the trouble of reading the book and I can tell the committee what you think.' The Committee of Management met on 6 December and not surprisingly found there was 'no useful action they could take on general principles'.

Algernon Methuen was sixty years old by this time and had

been ill for many years. Swinnerton accuses him of having 'ceased ... to pioneer and ... begun to think of safety'. *The Rainbow* was published in America in December with more excisions, of which Lawrence wrote: 'They are not many: yet they make me sad and angry.' They included the passage which had worried Carton. Meanwhile, and before the storm broke over *The Rainbow*, Lawrence had published 'England, My England' in the *English Review*. This story, with its title parodying a poem by Methuen author W. E. Henley, was based on the Meynell family and contained a mean little sketch of Percy Lucas, E. V.'s brother, who was married to one of the daughters of Wilfred Meynell. It would have been unlikely to endear Lawrence to E. V. Lucas at the crucial moment of the seizure and trial. E. V. was devoted to his brother who, though forty, volunteered and was killed in 1916, causing Lawrence temporarily to 'wish that story at the bottom of the sea'.

The Lawrences suffered in the ensuing months but were eventually to emerge with money and reputation from his writings. The damage to the firm was more lasting. Algernon was used to living a little dangerously in the matter of obscenity and fiction. In September 1914 he had written to Sir Frederick Macmillan rejecting a proposal by Harrods that publishers should take back 'dirty books'. He had suggested that the proposal was of less importance to Macmillans 'than to us for you are very cautious and not likely to run into indecencies.' He felt that Methuen authors would find any such proposal unacceptable and that they were being penalised: 'You know how sensitive authors are.' Clearly, I think, pressure, probably political, was brought on him to abandon *The Rainbow*, but the lasting effect on the company was to be a very severe reduction in the number of fiction titles and what looks like a deliberate shying away from difficult new work that might cause problems, though whether this is also because such authors were on their part withdrawing from Methuen it's hard to say. If so, it points up the significance when in 1922 Algernon wrote to Bennett saying how much he admired *Mr Prohack* and hoping that Bennett wouldn't desert the firm. Bennett himself was clearly dissatisfied with Methuen's running of the company and hoped for better things, as he wrote to Pinker when E. V. Lucas took over on Algernon's death. By 1920 the fiction list, once the pillar on which Methuen's reputation had been built, was dominated by Westerns, the Tarzan books of Edgar Rice Burroughs and Fu Man Chu thrillers by Sax Rohmer.

A look at what else was being published by the firm alongside *The Rainbow* in 1915 and 1916 points up its position as a sore thumb, beside old established names like Pett Ridge, Birmingham and Hope; indeed it must have been the support of Pinker and Bennett that got it into the list at all. The war consumed not only men and armaments but huge quantities of books. Those who in peacetime are too busy to read often

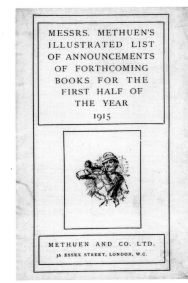

turn to poetry and fiction in particular, as indeed they do to music, to try to cope with the unfamiliar and with the mixture of fear, doubt and boredom that war brings. People need to be encouraged to fight and to be given hope that they or, if not they personally, something in which they have a part will survive. What this something is will vary from the immediately personal, lover or child, to the personalised abstractions of country, nature and god. Because the audience for poetry and fiction is suddenly greatly enlarged by the access of thousands of people who have no or little skill or training in reading, then those things which are most accessible are necessarily the most popular.

Methuen made an increasing profit during the war by supplying this need, which, once the forces of war were set in motion, becomes a legitimate craving if the human psyche is to survive. The list contains war poetry, novels, personal accounts and trench humour, as well as more academic and military appraisals of what is happening. Inevitably there is some Kaiser-bashing and self-justification. Atrocity stories were circulating freely, as well as the gallows humour of war jokes, but it was still largely possible for the British to distinguish good Germans, those they had met on holiday before the war, from bad ones,

(*left*) A. P. Herbert

(*right*) John Oxenham

the Prussian military caste, E. V. Lucas personifies this in a character in his epistolary novel *The Vermilion Box*, published in 1916, and dedicated to his dead brother Percy, whom Lawrence had protrayed so belittlingly in 'England, My England'.

The narrator's voice or attitudes seem to be embodied in the character of Richard Haven, the bachelor–philosopher and Mr Fix-It of the group of people the narrative follows for the first two years of the war. It's easy to see how far these opinions or assumptions often are from D. H. Lawrence's. 'By the way, I wonder what are the feelings of the conscientious objector as he gazes upon these poor but cheery one-legged and one-armed and blinded soldiers. I do not envy him his exclusion from any community with them,' Haven writes to his sister.

Nevertheless, Lucas resists the most common panacea of the war, the flight into religion, which was supplied by one of Methuen's most prolific and popular authors, John Oxenham, whose daughter Elsie was to become an equally prolific and popular author of girls' school stories. Lucas writes of the sinking of the *Lusitania* in his Haven persona: 'Christianity having failed so dismally (or would half the world be at each others' throats like this?) is it not time to try something else? Some religion of humanity ...' The hero's level-headed girl-friend expresses the same view when she writes: 'since the war it has been more perplexing still with the Germans and ourselves equally claiming our successes to be due to God's goodness'.

Judging from the popularity of Oxenham's religious poetry, the outpouring of a khaki Patience Strong, Lucas was deceiving himself when he believed that zeppelins raining death from the sky had dethroned God from heaven, but that wasn't his only miscalculation. He believed that the soldiers would be little changed by their experiences: '... I doubt if there will be much of it [change].... Most men, I imagine will bring back what they took out; war will be only skin deep.' Ironically, his truest prediction, which is meant not to be believed but to be merely doom-mongering, comes from the pessimistic George Wiston, whose function in the novel is to represent those who constantly criticise the conduct of the war and spread despondency, a perennial character that was to reappear in fiction and film during the Second World War, had been inveighed against by Queen Elizabeth I and is perhaps an abiding manifestation of our national character. Speaking of when the war is over, Wiston forecasts:

> After that there will be a period of intense depression, during which the great mass of people are realizing to their surprize and mortification that the millenium is not instant. Then there will be the gradual disbanding of a large part of the army, and the reluctance or inability of the men who have tasted blood, so to speak, to resume

their old tame lives. These will have to be dealt with, as well as the women, the substitutes for the more amenable ones, thrown thus out of employment. And all the while a very high rate of taxation will have to be maintained . . . .

The mention of women brings me to one of the most attractive of Lucas's attitudes, no doubt reflected in as well as reflecting the increasing numbers of women in publishing houses. Haven's sister Helen writes of her young cousin:

> If the Kaiser had never got on his hind legs she would merely be playing tennis and staying with friends, and burrowing in *Vogue* and all the rest of it. But now she has some clerical job at twenty-five shillings a week, eight hours a day. At the National Portrait Gallery of all places! . . . All around her, she says, are portraits of national highbrows, and hardly a woman among them . . . .

Haven himself approves: 'An independence will have come to her that she has woefully lacked – ranging her on the administrative side with French women, and self-reliantly with the Americans – and the Turks among us won't like it, but will have to put up with it.' In this case Lucas is more progressive than the deeply ingrained Turk, Lawrence, for whom women were largely best seen under the Anglo-Saxon term which translates 'wife' as 'dear bed companion'.

Yet in the end it's the irritating blindness of Lucas's style which, when set against the energy of Lawrence, keeps him among the Georgians along with the rest of the Methuen authors of the period, even including Hueffer and Conrad, who are structurally rather than verbally modernist. Since Lucas was himself a reader for the firm and a director, his influence must have been all-pervasive and his taste must clearly have chimed with that of Algernon Methuen. He must therefore be seen as partly responsible for the increasing blandness and reactionariness of the firm's list, even though Arnold Bennett saw him as full of ideas for change on the old man's death in 1924.

It would have been satisfying to discover a lost brilliance among the plethora of war poetry which the firm published, but none of it stands out. The weight of Kipling, of course, lies very heavy and some of the verse is firmly in his mode but without his ear or his demotic daring. Charles Foxcroft is a pale version of Grenfell and Brooke; Herbert Trench reaches the apotheosis of the Georgian in his 'Ode from Italy', and there are several others to keep him company: Alice Buxton, Llewellyn Bullock, Hope Fairfax Taylor, Octavia Gregory. It's hard now to imagine that the closing lines from Trench's 'Ode from Italy', to give just one example, are contemporary with 'The Love Song of J. Alfred Prufrock'.

... the ancient iron summit in his shroud
Of radiance, every pike and bastion dour
Belted with awe of glacier and crevasse,
Floats up, transfigured at this limpid hour,
A new acropolis of morning rosed,
A walled and heavenly city clear as glass –
Aerial, Lighter than a branch in flower –
An absolute but of our strifes composed.

The influence of Milton and Miltonic Keats clog the lines.

Between 1910 and 1920 a gulf was opened by modernism in literature into which dozens of Georgian poets tumbled as in some medieval doom painting. In retrospect Eliot's and Pound's innovations seem as necessary and inevitable as rock and roll was to be for the popular music of the 1950s. Such a revolution, however, also inevitably poses the question of the importance of theory to the practice of literature. One of Methuen's most serious poets is himself an interesting case.

Alfred Noyes is known now largely for his much anthologised narrative poem 'The Highwayman', which some of us can still chant all the way through, with its romantic story and galloping beat. Noyes had undoubted talent, perhaps too great a facility, but he was hampered by his fear of licence, a need for 'law' which, translated into poetic form, meant the continuation of strict rhyming stanzas and poetic diction.

In 1915 Methuen published his *A Salute From the Fleet*, containing some sixty poems. 'The Repeal' sets out his philosophical stance.

> I dreamed the Eternal had repealed
>     His cosmic code of law last night.
> Our prayers had made the Unchanging yield
>     Caprice was King from depth to height.
>
> On Beachy Head a shouting throng
>     Had fired a beacon to proclaim
> Their licence. With unmeasured song
>     They proved it, dancing in the flame.
>
> They quarrelled. One desired the sun,
>     And one desired the stars to shine.
> They closed and wrestled and burned as one,
>     And the white chalk grew red as wine.
>
> The furnace licked and purred and rolled
>     A laughing child held up its hands
> Like dreadful torches, dropping gold;
>     For pain was dead at their commands.
>
> Painless and wild as clouds they burned,
>     Till the restricted Rose of Day
> With all its glorious laws returned,
>     And the wind blew their ashes away.

Noyes's one-act play about the German invasion of Belgium, *Rada*, which Methuen also published for him in 1915, is on the whole more successful, although tinged wih melodrama at its big moments. It opposes German intellectualism to British provincialism, with a side swipe at 'what the age wants – realism!', while itself uneasily employing a naturalistic mode in the story of a Belgian mother's attempt to save her twelve-year-old daughter from rape by the German soldiery, which is only achieved by shooting her child and herself. The German view as presented expressed the traditional British distrust of the intellectual, but in this case from a writer who can only do so by, however briefly and unwillingly, taking the part of the intellectual.

> TARRASCH: It was brutal I confess; but better than British
> hypocrisy, eh? There was something great about it,
> like the neighing of the satyrs in the Venusberg
> music.... They were beginning to find out the prov-
> incialism of their creeds in England. The pessimism
> of Schopenhauer had taught them much; and if it
> had not been for this last treachery, this last rid-
> iculous outburst of the middle-class mind on behalf
> of what they call honour, we should have continued
> to tolerate (if not to enjoy), in Berlin, those plays by
> Irishmen which expose so wittily the inferior *Kultur*,
> the shrinking from reality, of their (for the most part)
> not intellectual people.'

Noyes typifies the artistic manifestation of innate British conservatism and dislike of the unknown which can so easily be exploited for jingoistic purposes. It was a strand which was to continue to run alongside modernism, and still in the late twentieth century accompanies its extension into modernism's so-called successors, with the result that since the First World War the division in English literature into traditional, experimental and popular has become increasingly marked.

Methuen's most accomplished poet at this period, Kipling always excepted, is technically A. P. Herbert, one of the writers who had come to the list from *Punch*, undoubtedly, like A. A. Milne, through the influence of Lucas. The humorous element in Methuen publishing, although not separate in the catalogue at this period, had been strong from the beginning of the century – both in children's and adult books. Herbert's *The Bomber Gipsy*, under the guise of irony, is able to be concrete and specific about war, once again in a very British way, one which has always used the various modes of comedy to deal with, and often in the process laugh off, problems and difficult emotions. Herbert's poems are good-natured grouses, the 'poetic' diction is comic, taking the edge off the very real bitterness with the sheer confidence of the verse-making.

O God of War is this the end?
   O Mars who made the shameful Hun,
Is this the final shame you send
   To show us we have fairly won?
   A thing that fairly takes the bun,
That turns our golden deeds to dross.
   O Vimy Ridge and O Verdun –
*The A.D.C. has got the Cross*!

The collection belongs to the last year of the war when the romance had gone out of it all in the muck of Flanders and, when Herbert forgets or feels no obligation to be humorous, as in 'After the Battle', which was first published in the *New Statesman* rather than *Punch*, the pain is intense and vividly conveyed.

You will come up in your capacious car
   To find your heroes sulking in the rain,
To tell us how magnificent we are,
   And how you hope we'll do the same again . . .

We who must mourn those spaces in the Mess,
   And somehow fill those hollows in the heart,
We do not want your Sermon on Success
   Your greasy benisons on Being Smart.

We only want to take our wounds away
   To some warm village where the tumult ends,
And drowsing in the sunshine many a day,
   Forget our aches, forget that we had friends . . .

THE SECRET
BATTLE
*by*
A. P. HERBERT

THE
FOUNTAIN
LIBRARY    2.6ᵈ

Herbert was also to produce Methuen's finest piece of war prose fiction in *The Secret Battle*, first published in 1919 after he had been wounded and returned to civilian life. It's the story of the destruction of youthful romance and, eventually, of the young Harry Penrose himself, whose nerve goes and who is shot for cowardice. The events are related by Benson, an older regular officer, in a blankly formal prose, which nevertheless has all the concrete precision of first-hand observation. The descriptions of life on the Gallipoli campaign could probably not have been published while the war was still on without incurring the charge of undermining public morale. In their finely controlled disgust, however, they are as powerful as some of the best of the war poetry.

By 1919, when the public itself was sick of the whole enterprise and longed for peace, such a publication was sure to find an audience, but there is another very fine piece of writing, first published in 1917, which is the infantryman's Great War equivalent of Richard Hilary's *The Last Enemy*, published in 1941. Like Hilary, the author Bernard Adams was to go back into the fighting, after being wounded, and die almost at once.

*Nothing of Importance* is a brilliant first-hand evocation of trench warfare, in which the author moves gradually from the position of romantic excitement to the full realisation of what is happening to him and to those around him, to civilisation itself.

> What made war so cruel, was the force that compelled you to go on. After a factory explosion you cleared up things and then took every precaution to prevent its recurrence. But in war you did the opposite, you used all your energies to make more explosions. You killed and went on killing; you saw men die around you, and you deliberately went on with the thing that would cause more of your friends to die. You were placed in an arena, and made to fight the beasts; and if you killed one beast, there were more waiting and more and more. And above the arena, out of it secure, looked down the glittering eyes of the men who had placed you there; cruel, relentless eyes, that went on glittering while the mouths expressed admiration for your impossible struggles, and pity for your fate.

There's no trace here of the fustian which even Herbert still has an echo of. It is the truly modern voice, free, although Adams intended to become a missionary in India, of the cadences and inversions and rhetorical questions of the nineteenth-century pulpit which continued to affect even the writing of a spy story like *Tipperary Tommy* or the Williamsons' romance, *The War Wedding*.

Adams, unfortunately for literature as well as himself, was only twenty-six when he was killed, having been born in the same year as A. P. Herbert. The first-hand account is of course in many ways easier for the amateur, and success in it doesn't always mean that its author can go on to become a professional writer. There are, however, other such accounts in the Methuen list to compare with *Nothing of Importance* and to help form an estimate of the writer's potential. Roughly parallel to it is C. A. L. Brownlow's *The Breaking of the Storm*, a workmanlike account of the first months of the war in Europe, published in 1918, but the prose gives no feeling that there is a literary sensibility that might go on to deal with other subjects.

The most unusual account comes from the Jewish journalist Israel Cohen, interned in the Ruhleben prison camp in the early weeks of the war along with over four thousand other British nationals who had been caught on the continent for a variety of reasons. In spite of the unusualness of his material there is a curious superficiality in his approach, except when he is dealing with the various manifestations of pro- and anti-semitism among both fellow prisoners and guards. In bleak retrospect after the holocaust, there's a terrible irony in Cohen's complaints about having to do ordinary domestic chores in a concentration camp.

---

## NOTHING OF IMPORTANCE

### BY
### BERNARD ADAMS

T HIS book presents a series of pictures of life at the Front during a period when 'Nothing of Importance' (from a military point of view) occurred. Scenes in billets, incidents in the trenches, sniping, mines and patrols, bring the reader face to face with the pathos and the dreariness, the heroism and the humour, of war. Everything described is true in all details, while the psychology of war serves throughout as a background. Within a month from the completion of the MS. the author was struck down while leading his men in an attack, and he died a few hours later.

METHUEN & CO. LTD. LONDON

We swept our horsebox every morning, we blacked our boots, we shook our straw sacks and bedding, we cleaned our crockery under the stable-taps, and made our knives bright by thrusting them into the sandy soil... But it was not long before the miserable monotony of these occupations palled upon us, and we employed men at rates from one to two marks a week, to relieve us of such work.

In the end he has a 'blackie', one of the British colonials interned in their own barrack, as his servant.

C. W. Chamberlain in uniform
(front row centre)

The hierarchical view to which he gives such unconscious expression is one which would itself be severely battered in the trenches, but the unquestioning acceptance of class and racial divisions was already there as a weapon for fascist exploitation in the attitude which saw nothing wrong in allocating occupations of 'miserable monotony' to women, blacks and the lower orders. Israel Cohen's poor health enabled him to be repatriated after a little less than two years' internment. Perhaps it's only hindsight that makes the danger inherent in the rampant anti-semitism which he describes appear so much more obviously threatening than it seems to have been to those who experienced it at the time.

With hindsight too, and in the light of Methuen's other publications, the *Rainbow* affair also becomes more explicable.

It seems to me that it was probably less Lawrence's German wife and his known anti-war stance than, as the records indicate, his portrayal of female sexuality which caused the violent reactions to the book, the cries of 'filth' and demands for suppression. It was crucial that the young men at the front should have an image of pure and faithful women to carry with them and fight for as a counterpoint to the real filth and brutality they were forced to face. A. P. Herbert understood this very well when he dedicated *The Bomber Gipsy* to the waiting wives, and when he described Harry Penrose's wife in *The Secret Battle*: 'She was a dark, gentle little person with brown and rather sorrowful eyes. When I first saw her I thought, "She was never meant to be a soldier's wife", but after we had talked a little I added, "But she is a good one".'

The true cause of offence in *The Rainbow* was the suggestion that women were not only sexual beings in their own right but might be emotionally and sexually self-sufficient, offering an alternative to the heterosexual establishment for which young men were being asked to suffer and die. Male homosexuality in the non-explicit forms of soldierly comradeship was acceptable, as when, for example, Bernard Adams writes of a fellow officer, Davidson: 'He used to come in and stroke your hair if you were bad-tempered. Somehow he reminded me of a cat purring; or perhaps his hair and his smile had something to do with it? Oh who can define what they love in those they love?'

Two of Methuen's sevenpenny novels

It was female homosexuality that was a threat and was singled out for special notice by the critics and the Society of Authors' adviser, yet another irony given that Lawrence, the aggressive heterosexual, had entitled the chapter 'Shame'.

By 1919 paper had risen to four times its pre-war price, some mills would only accept tentative orders, printers were restive and binders were increasing their charges with almost every order. Nevertheless, the company continued to make a profit and the dividend rose to 9 per cent for 1917. Sir Algernon, as he now was, congratulated the staff on their efforts and loyalty and this included, he said, 'that part belonging to the gentler sex who had done much'. By the 1919 AGM he was able to welcome those who had returned safely and announce that sales in 1918 had made a record, 'though there was so large an amount of money in circulation at the moment that values had become rather fictitious'. It was thirty years since the founding of the firm on the promise of a book by Hensley Henson 'so slow in gestation that it had not been delivered yet'. He reminded them that the first book to be published, *Derrick Vaughan, Novelist* by Edna Lyall, was still selling, and announced that in celebration of the thirtieth anniversary he intended to make a further distribution of shares among the staff. Methuen, like Britain, had come through.

Hermann Struck
1920

# FOUR

# The Apeman and relativity
## 1919–1929

Many of the Methuen staff had been killed in the war and three others who had been unfit for military service died soon after, two of Spanish flu and another of a virulent diabetes, perhaps proving the efficiency of the army medics. Nevertheless some men did return, and many of the girls left, but no decision to go back to an all-male staff was ever taken and some stayed on, only leaving to get married.

C. W. Chamberlain returned and, no doubt replacing the son they had never had, became Algernon Methuen's confidant to the exclusion of the irascible managing director George Webster. Chamberlain had joined the RASC, although nearly forty, in 1917 and been wounded, but not severely enough to be invalided home. In his quiet way Methuen was grooming him to take over from Webster when the time came.

*The Secret Battle*, which Methuen bought for £50, was a commercial flop although 'read all night' by Lloyd George, who commended it to the then Secretary of State for War, Winston Churchill. The public wanted war either romanticised, as in John Oxenham's *1914*, or in the small doses of Ernest Raymond's *Tell England*. They had had enough of death and failure and certainly didn't want to be reminded that men had been shot by their own side.

In one of the few extant anecdotes about Sir Algernon, A. P. Herbert makes it clear that his chief concern was to keep the firm afloat and rebuild it successfully in the changed conditions post-war. 'It doesn't cost you money to write a book,' he told the young author. 'It does cost us money to publish it. Books don't grow on trees. I wonder if you have the slightest idea what our bill for paper was last year, Mr Herbert?' Writers are of course used to the suggestion that their time and labour cost nothing and Herbert left the office 'almost ready to apologise for having written a book'.

Nevertheless, after a short stab at a legal career, he returned to Methuen, this time under the protection of A. P. Watt. Now catching the flavour of the times, he wrote a thriller with comic overtones and a Thames setting, *The House By The River*. He

# RELATIVITY

## THE SPECIAL AND THE GENERAL THEORY

### A POPULAR EXPOSITION

BY

## A. EINSTEIN

TRANSLATED BY

## ROBERT W. LAWSON, D.Sc.

IN this book, which is written for the average reader, Prof. Einstein explains his famous theory of Relativity, which has so excited the scientific world. The Einstein law has been accepted by astronomers and physicists as an epoch-making discovery. Up to the present Newton's law of gravitation has been universally accepted, but the new theory goes further, and the present book is intended, as far as possible, to give an exact insight into the Theory of Relativity to those readers who, from a general scientific and philosophical point of view, are interested in the theory, but who are not conversant with the mathematical apparatus of theoretical physics. The author has spared himself no pains in his endeavour to present the main ideas in the simplest and most intelligible form.

## METHUEN & CO. LTD. LONDON

also offered what was to become an increasing staple of the Methuen list, a collection of humorous pieces from his *Punch* writings, *Light Articles Only*.

The title is a fair indication of the public's needs, at least interpreted by Methuen after being so badly burned over *The Rainbow*. The war, of course, didn't immediately drop out of the list. There was a book about the war debt and how to pay it and E. V. Lucas's humorous account *Quoth the Raven* in 1919. Both Anthony Hope and Richard Bagot used the war as a background to a thriller and there were half a dozen non-fiction books dealing with different aspects of it: its causes, the war at sea and in Italy, and with the London gunners. Two books on Greece and Poland set out to explain some of the results of the Armistice.

By spring 1920 there were only two non-fiction treatments of the war and a novel – *How They Did It* by Gerald O'Donovan, about wartime profiteering – an even greater flop than *The Secret Battle*, which had at least reached a second edition by 1927, while O'Donovan's book had vanished from the catalogue. What were to be the main supports of the list for the next decade were, however, two at least in full view and one signalled. Ironically, the most prestigious book on the list was by a scientist of German birth, then at the University of Berlin.

A new educational manager, A. Watson Bain, was appointed in 1919. He lasted only four years and was frequently at loggerheads with the managing director, Webster, but he began the development of the educational, scientific and technical side of the firm which was to be its great strength and eventually to be carried on by the almost legendary E. V. Rieu.

Science and education had been given a boost by the war and the new Education Act of 1918. It was realised that Britain lagged behind her late enemy both in elementary education and research. Work that had been bottled up in German universities by the hostilities now became available, and Methuen secured the plum in this rich mixture: Einstein. 'Einstein's Great Book' as it is described in the catalogue for 1920, *Relativity: The Special and the General Theory*, 'marks the commencement of a new era in scientific and philosophical research'. Just because it was such a *coup* it appears at the beginning of the Announcements, under the heading General Literature instead of further along in its rightful place with the other Scientific and Technical books, and it was Methuen himself who had said to C. W. Chamberlain with great excitement that he thought he was 'onto something'.

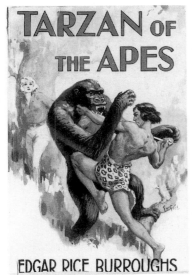

As well as these two categories there was Sport and Travel; Philosophy, Economics and Politics; Educational and Fiction, now dominated by Edgar Rice Burroughs with both the Tarzan and the Martian series, beginning with *Tarzan of the Apes* in 1917, and *A Princess of Mars* in 1919. Increasingly, the list showed a tendency towards genre fiction, with not only science

fiction and fantasy of the Burroughs school but Westerns, of whom B. M. Bower was the most prolific exponent, and detective and thriller novels. More serious literature was represented by reprints of Conrad, Bennett and Oscar Wilde.

At the same time prices of books were rising. By 1920 new novels cost, at eight shillings and sixpence, the equivalent of a fifth of the average weekly industrial wage, or £40 in the 1980s. Clearly the target for new fiction wasn't the industrial or agricultural worker but the middle classes, and then largely through the circulating libraries. These figures help to explain Arnold Bennett's dissatisfaction with Methuen for having 'got out of the sixpenny market where many of his northern readers might be likely to be found.

Just as interesting a comment on the post-war years, and also, I believe, on the influence of cinema on fiction, is the fact that middle-class readers were prepared to pay so much for a Western or detective novel. All sources attest to the very shrewd business sense of Algernon Methuen. He had rightly gauged the needs of this new age for diversion and education: Tarzan and Einstein. Methuen's profits continued to rise and were only interrupted by a strike in 1921 which seems, although the memoirs and minute books aren't specific, to be, like the later one in 1925, by the packers. 1920 had been a record year for profits but six and a half weeks of strike, during which it seems as if the clerical staff had kept things going, for they were congratulated on their 'esprit de corps and loyalty' in the speech by the managing director at the April 1922 Annual General Meeting, was bound to have some effect, though not as much as the management initially feared.

The union involved was the Paperworkers, and no doubt the rising prices had made them feel that they too might have a share in the annually increasing profits. Profit was now very much Methuen's concern and, as chief reader and soon-to-be chairman, E. V. Lucas must bear a great responsibility for the nature of the list. Algernon Methuen must still have been largely responsible for the educational side. One of his final and most influential acts was the appointment in 1923 of E. V. Rieu as educational manager. Methuen certainly solicited T. S. Eliot's *The Sacred Wood* for 1920 and produced his own anthology of modern poetry, which was a modest but consistent best-seller, a few months after. However, E. V. Lucas's own work appears unflaggingly on both the fiction and general literature lists, and it must be queried whether there isn't something rather distasteful, if not even culturally undesirable, in a publisher massively promulgating his own work in this way.

Cinema had created a new interest in America, and American books play an increasingly important part in the new publications. Both writers and editors, as is clear from the writings of A. P. Herbert and Alfred Noyes, and references in the minute books, visited the States. Perhaps Algernon saw in

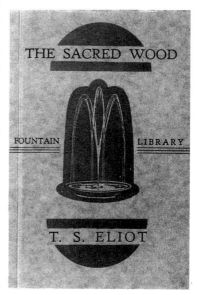

THE SACRED WOOD

FOUNTAIN LIBRARY

T. S. ELIOT

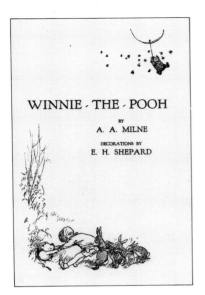

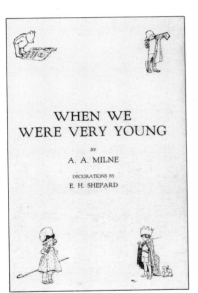

Eliot's classical literary values an antidote to some of his own transatlantic activity from a writer who had made the journey the other way, or a new way of making the hamburger pay for the caviare.

Agents must have realised that Methuen weren't to be tempted by the modernists. A manuscript book for 1926 which lists those received, from whom, by whom read and their fate, contains few names still current fifty years later, except for the non-fiction classics like Einstein. Among those rejected was, however, one money-spinner: the Kai Lung books by Ernest Bramah, although Methuen was already publishing *The Wallet of Kai Lung*, while another by someone who was already a popular Methuen author, A. A. Milne's *Winnie-the-Pooh*, was, luckily for the firm, accepted. Since *When We Were Very Young* had already been an astounding success in 1924, lifting the firm's profits to a new record, this was hardly surprising.

In 1926 Methuen returned nine books to Curtis Brown in thirteen days, including a George Gissing reissue and Ford Madox Hueffer (Ford)'s *Ladies Whose Bright Eyes*. As usual in publishing, the rejection even of books from established agents outnumber the acceptances, including those dubbed 'for revision', almost immeasurably. In the first week in May 1928 forty-three books were logged as received from the second to the fifth; two were accepted outright and one returned for revision. Curtis Brown, as the agent for Edgar Rice Burroughs, might have expected favourable treatment but doesn't appear to have got it.

The Tarzan phenomenon deserves, I think, a little more study. Part of Tarzan's success must be due to the sheer quantity: the addiction, once established, could be constantly fed. Seven titles were published in the first three years alone. Yet there is more to it than numbers. Tarzan is a genuine folk-creation, an image with a strong appeal to the human psyche. After the filth and degradation of the Great War he is presented as essentially an innocent whose only weapon, in contrast to the murderous armoury of so-called civilisation, is the hunting knife and his own strength. He kills for food and to protect his own. He is nature's aristocrat for whom the right moral choice is almost instinctive, even when he carries off Jane and contemplates rape like his forest cousins. He provides an escapist balm to nerves shattered by a world war and industrial collapse. Tarzan is the other side of those roaring twenties which A. P. Herbert evoked in *The Old Flame* and its descriptions of the new dancing craze which Methuen was to do its bit to fuel in *Dos and Don'ts of Dancing* and *Ballroom Dancing*, with its evocative black-and-white art deco illustrations, both published in 1925. *Dos and Don'ts* also extended to dining and decorating as well as rabbit breeding, elocution, Mah Jong, beekeeping and 'the well-dressed woman's'. The series conveys an impression of a *nouveau* if not *riche*, at least *comfortable*, lacking in self-confidence and eager for self-improvement.

A. P. Herbert's *The Old Flame* also explores the new morality of partner-swapping and a hectic London social life of clubs and cafés, in marked contrast to the simple lifestyle of Tarzan's jungle nest. These new social mores are complementary to the great advances in science and technology. The theory of relativity itself, when translated into the moral and social sphere, added to the sensations of impermanence and instability in contrast to the pre-war world during which Methuen itself had been built up. The idea that truth wasn't the ordered Newtonian universe but something that shifted with the view-point of the beholder, was, indeed, multi-dimensional, itself reflected the shifting post-war world.

The greatest change of all for the firm was to come in 1924. It seems too to have been quite unexpected. First Sabine Baring-Gould died, then Marie Corelli and, on 20 September, Algernon Methuen himself. His own last book, published in 1922, had expressed one of his lifelong interests: *An Alpine ABC and List of Easy Rock Plants*, whose advertisement in the catalogue included the words: 'Nothing is included which cannot be grown by the amateur'.

He had made a publishing house grow, yet in a sense had remained an amateur while overseeing every detail of the business. His dissatisfaction with the managing director had also grown to the point where he effectively dismissed Webster by the terms of his will, fearing perhaps that with himself gone no one else would be strong enough to cope with him. Accordingly, E. V. Lucas became chairman and Methuen's own favourite, C. W. Chamberlain, managing director. There were those who believed, according to E. J. Roberts, who himself decided to leave the company at this time, that Webster had been the real power while Methuen was only the figurehead, but Roberts makes it unequivocal that Methuen was the true director and creative force while Webster was a hard-working and meticulous right-hand man.

Lucas was chosen as chairman by the directors; Chamberlain was Methuen's posthumous appointment and Webster's sense of grievance comes through strongly, in spite of E. V. Lucas's muted attempt at eulogy in the minutes of the 1925 AGM. 'For thirty-two years Mr Webster was Sir Algernon's right hand, and we all know how vigilant and devoted he was and how intimately he was concerned with every branch of the business.'

Algernon was commemorated by his wife with portrait busts in marble and bronze which she presented to the firm. Lucas wrote a privately printed memoir of him and in his first AGM speech as chairman spoke of the sense of loss and regret 'both corporate and personal'. At the board meeting at which he was elected chairman Lucas referred to the founding of the firm as 'one of the most remarkable feats in the history of publishing. I doubt if any other man ... could have done it under any conditions and certainly not with so few changes of staff, such

A COMPLETE
AND ILLUSTRATED
CATALOGUE OF BOOKS
PUBLISHED BY
METHUEN & CO. LTD.
LONDON
1923

FOUNTAIN COURT, TEMPLE

METHUEN AND CO. LTD.
36 ESSEX STREET, LONDON, W.C. 2

easy good humour, so much apparent detachment covering so real and constant a vigilance and so little ostentation.'

SIR·ALGERNON·METHUEN·BT·
BORN·1856·DIED·1924·FOUNDER·OF
METHUEN·AND·CO·PUBLISHERS·1889

The memorial plaque to Sir Algernon at 36 Essex Street

Webster's resignation came to the board ten days later. It was brusque and gave no reason. In accepting it Lucas spoke of 'his knowledge of technical detail, his quick grasp of essentials and his unfailing accessibility' which had 'made for himself a name wherever, either in England or America, the art of publishing is discussed'. Roberts makes it clear that his 'lashing tongue could arouse deep resentment. He was respected for his energy and ability but he was not liked.' He delivered the monthly pay packets personally for each member of the clerical staff, which must have given him many opportunities to exercise his reputation as a martinet.

The next business at this meeting was to fix the salaries of the board. Lucas was voted £1,200 a year as chairman, plus

£800 as reader: £2,000 in all. Chamberlain was awarded £1,300 and Frederick Muller, as assistant managing director, was given £1,100. Killby, who was head of production or 'Q and B' (quire and binding, as it was called) became a second assistant manager at £1,000 a year. In contrast to Webster, Killby was very popular, although no less efficient in his very important department. 'A wit and an inveterate practical joker…: A very kindly man at heart', he had also 'an ice-cool brain. He was seldom if ever rattled.'

Q and B was an elaborate operation in the days when small editions were constantly ordered for immediate delivery, warehoused and despatched from the premises in Essex Street. It was for this reason that the packers, who were regarded as very low in the scale of publishing life, were nevertheless so vital. They arrived an hour earlier than the clerical staff in order to sweep and clean the premises. They worked from eight to six and eight to one on Saturdays with an hour for lunch and no other break. They were given a week's paid holiday a year and were paid weekly by Chamberlain.

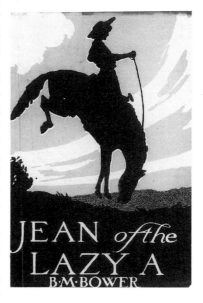

Algernon Methuen's death and the subsequent changes coincided with the growing industrial unrest, both in the book trade itself and in British society generally, which was to culminate in the General Strike two years later. In this context the rising prices, profits and the large salaries awarded themselves by the new board are significant. Webster was given a lump sum of £5,000 and an annual pension of £900. In contrast, Henry Christmas, Algernon's private secretary, was awarded £200, and the widow of E.M. Ingram, a former employee and shareholder, continued to be paid at £78 a year. The average wage in 1924 was just over £100 a year. In 1925 E.V. Lucas was also voted three per cent per annum on the net profits in addition to his salary on a five-year contract.

Things began to go wrong when it came to implementing other parts of Sir Algernon's will. The trustees of the estate tried to argue that the £5 for every year of service to each employee was only to date from the founding of the limited company in 1910, not, as he had always clearly intended, from the beginning of each individual's service. The sum needed to bring the legacies up to this was £970, half of which was in the event paid by Lady Methuen herself.

The packers went on strike again in 1925, part of a concerted action by the Paperworkers' Union to improve pay and conditions throughout the industry. Once again the clerical staff helped to break the strike; the existing packing staff were sacked and replaced by new workers. E.V. Lucas, in his address to the AGM, recorded that the result of the strike was 'the total disappearance of the Paperworkers' Union from all Publishing Houses that are members of the Book Trade Employers Federation' which Methuen had joined. The directors' minutes record that the company signed an agreement for concerted

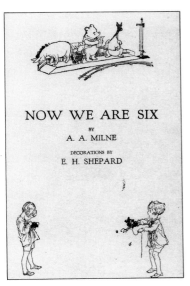

action with the Federation 'where that may be necessary to protect their interests' in March 1927. One good result of the strike was the publishers' recognition that some kind of scheme of Pensions and Death Benefit Assurance was necessary for the packing staff and Methuen adopted this in 1927, paying half the premium to the Metropolitan Life Assurance Society.

Under Sir Algernon's will, his estate was to go at his wife's death mainly to Berkhamsted School and Wadham College. Three trustees had been appointed to look after the estate and had been given the option of selling at any time that seemed to them advantageous. Perhaps as a result of the unrest in 1925–6 and because of the high profitability of the company on the A. A. Milne boom, they decided to exercise this option in 1926.

The company was thrown into a chaos of confusion and doubt as a result. An action in the High Court had been taken some two or three years before by the legatees of the Northcliffe shares in the *Daily Mail*, where it was alleged that the trustees had taken a lower price than they could have got. Consequently the Methuen sale was finally to be decided by a judge in chambers, but not before a great deal of to-ing and fro-ing had taken place.

The trustees might also have been alarmed by what appears in the AGM minutes for 1927 as 'one unfortunate enterprise' which had caused profits to be a little less than for 1926, a record year. This, I believe, was the publication late in 1926 of *My Early Life* by the ex-Kaiser William II at the amazing price of thirty shillings. Lucas and Muller had been in Berlin, presumably in pursuit of the German scientists whose work was the staple of the scientific section and who had perhaps been drawn to the list by Einstein's reputation. As well as a new work by him on *The Theory of the Brownian Movement*, there are books by Sommerfeld of the University of Munich on 'atomic physics', by Freundlich of Berlin and Ostwald of Leipzig, Nernst of Berlin and Raymond of Lausanne.

Lucas and Muller hadn't consulted the rest of the board about the Kaiser's memoirs. They said there had been no time, but Chamberlain and Killby felt that too much had been paid for it and forced the following resolution at the 26 July board meeting: 'Before a decision is arrived at with respect of any proportion of more than usual magnitude the consent of the board must be obtained.'

Whatever their reasons, the trustees decided late in 1926 that the time had come to sell Sir Algernon's shares in the company which were valued at £250,000. The directors, who had been hoping for what would now be called a management buy-out in order to secure the firm and the jobs of its directors and employees, spent the next three months, with the support of Lady Methuen, trying to devise a way of bringing this about in a flurry of letters, meetings and pencil calculations on bits of paper which still survive.

By July 1927 the matter was still unresolved. Two schemes
had been mooted and foundered largely because of the high
price put on the shares. The next was for a financier, Sir William
Berry, to buy all the shares and undertake to maintain the
status quo. At this point E. V. Lucas became ill, no doubt largely
because of the strain of the last six months, and was forced to
flee the country for a brief holiday to recover. He returned
recovered to take up the struggle. Sir William disappears from
the scene and the directors engaged a kind of businessman's
detective agency to investigate the credentials of several possible new buyers. Then in November 1927 the business was
suddenly taken off the market and both directors and trustees
agreed the wording of an announcement to this effect which
was sent to all the papers.

A staff outing to Kingston

> We are asked to give publicity to the statement of the
> directors of Messrs Methuen & Co., Ltd, of whom Mr E. V.
> Lucas is Chairman, that their business is not for sale and
> that the rumours that it is to be absorbed by any other
> firm are groundless. No change in character or personnel
> is contemplated by the firm.

Lady Methuen was herself relieved that things were now to
go on 'as at present which is *quite well* I think', as she wrote in
November in a charming letter to Frederick Muller, E. V. Lucas
having once again been driven abroad in search of health. It's
clear that she took a deep interest in the firm, referring to it as

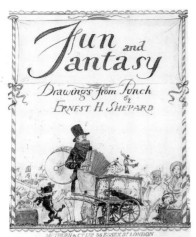

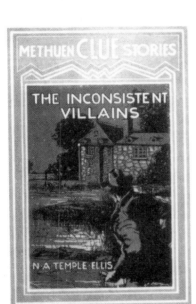

The winner of the first detective novel competition.

'we', asking for a copy of Einstein's *Relativity* for the *average* reader to be sent to a relative, Frank Bedford, and praising 'the charming illustrated catalogue of *our* [my italics] Xmas books. It is quite a feast of good things.'

Whether this cessation of activity was only a blind it's hard to tell, but by January 1928 the wheeling and dealing was in full swing again. Three more potential buyers appeared, including a Mr George Roberts who, having made a fortune in biscuits and felt, was willing to pay the trustees the full price of £2 15s a share and to guarantee the continuation of the *status quo* in the running of the business. After more intense negotiation, during which Lucas was in Portugal still recuperating, Roberts emerged as the new proprietor at a price of £3 1s per share.

At an Extraordinary General Meeting on 22 May, Lucas was able to announce the name of the new owner:

> Mr Roberts is not particularly interested in literature: he merely liked the idea of putting some of his money into an old established publishing firm of the highest reputation. Your directors have met him, and we found him more than ready to repose confidence in us, and therefore in you; and so far as we can tell as such an early stage, no change that could possibly affect anybody here for the worse is likely to occur.

Roberts himself wrote to Muller a week later: 'Strange, is it not? that the past and the present owner should have had in common the love of gardens in general and of rock gardens in particular.' He wasn't, however, to be an entirely sleeping proprietor, as Lucas had hoped, for he at once suggested a competition to find new detective writers. The change also necessitated the winding up and reflotation of the company as a public one, during which process Lucas and the other directors tried to get the commission or percentage of profit element in their salaries hardened into fixed salaries, but were told that that 'would do away with the incentive which is supposed to attach to the fact that part of such emolument should be the result of successful endeavour'.

The authors had to be persuaded, as is usual in such takeovers, to reassign their works to the new company. Most of the existing contracts were not terminable, but those that were represented 'a few of our best authors' including Kipling, Corelli, Anthony Hope and A. P. Herbert.

Lady Methuen herself died in 1928, perhaps affected by the long uncertainty and the eventual loss of the company which had been the Methuens' offspring and had given them their name. The public disclosure of the accounts which the sale had made necessary, accounts which Sir Algernon himself had always kept very close to his chest, showed that the company

had been doing extremely well, with profits running at an average of £30–40,000 over the last ten years, not just from publishing but also from very judicious investment.

On the publishing side, it has to be said that the money came largely from half a dozen identifiable bestselling authors, all of whom belong to Algernon Methuen's final years. Lucas was to claim at a later AGM that the management had continued to follow his precepts and practices. A later chairman, J. Alan White, has criticised this post-Methuen management for lack of policy, but there was little incentive for Lucas and Chamberlain to evolve an ethos of their own when they had inherited one that was working so well.

It's clear from an examination of the entries of manuscripts received for the last years of the 1920s that if exciting books were being written, they weren't being offered to the company. No genius who went on to publish elsewhere leaps to the eye except, ironically since Methuen were to publish him thirty years later, Bertolt Brecht, with four plays sent by his German publisher. There may, of course, have been lost masterpieces that never found a publisher at all but the very titles themselves suggest otherwise. If a work seemed promising it had to pass four readers: William Rowntree, H. C. Bailey, Ronald Knox and finally A. A. Milne. They regularly accepted each other's work, and when *The House At Pooh Corner* was delivered on 13 February 1928, it was sent, presumably without a reader's report, to the printers the following day. Among the refusals in March was, interestingly, a book by L. A. G. Strong, who was later to be the firm's chief literary adviser.

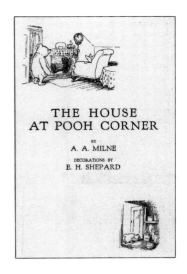

The Milne phenomenon, like the Tarzan one, finds, I believe, an explanation in the post-war desire for the lost innocence trampled to death in the trenches. The attested popularity with adults as well as children, of Rose Fyleman's fairy books like *Fairies and Chimneys*, springs partly from the same reaction which at its worst led to a sickeningly twee tone of voice and a resolute determination not to face the post-war realities of deepening depression and social unrest. Christopher Robin lives in a world of rickets, malnutrition and tuberculosis for the majority of the nation's children, yet nothing of it impinges on him. In contrast, Robert Louis Stevenson's *Child's Garden of Verses* are hatched with darker tones and the brilliance and variety of the poems make them a classic, not just a children's classic as Milne's books are.

Milne's involvement with Methuen had come about through the *Punch* connection and had been long and profitable before he became the Pooh megastar. It wasn't surprising that he would, after four such books, want to return to adult readers and eventually find what was a renewed career in the theatre, dramatising that other Methuen children's classic by Kenneth Grahame, *The Wind in the Willows*, as *Toad of Toad Hall*, which Methuen published in 1929. What is surprising is that in the

(*clockwise*) Rose Fyleman

P. G. Wodehouse

H. V. Morton

middle of all this work he could still find time to be Methuen's reader and final arbiter on the fate of so many books.

P. G. Wodehouse, of course another prolific *Punch* contributor, also fits what seems to be an overall policy of determined fictional light-heartedness with the series of 'Jeeves' books beginning in 1919. The firm's list had effectively split in two: the heavy side was kept for the bread and butter of education and science, while fiction was a diversionary froth which couldn't offend or disturb. there were to be no more *Rainbow*s, and this policy suited the new managing director, Chamberlain, whose passion was for sales, and Lucas's own lightweight style. By the end of the decade the General Literature section of the catalogue was some 160 pages with an average of ten books to a page. There were 56 pages of non-fiction series and only 19 pages of fiction.

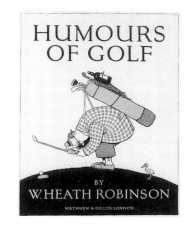

Among the series was one which also reflected the post-war search for conviction and stability in 'the present confusion', as the catalogue calls it. This was an examination of all the faiths, including the different varieties of Christianity. In the political field, too, post-war conditions were producing new parties offering their own solutions to the problems of unemployment and poverty, as people looked for conviction in this area of human activity with the old kingdoms broken and remade by the war. There was G. Prezzolini's *Fascism* in Autumn 1926, an early attempt to describe Mussolini's Italian reforms, and Leon Trotsky's *Towards Socialism or Capitalism*, both important works in the development of world politics, while 1928 produced *A History of the Jews in England* by A. Hyamson and *Republican Germany* by Quigley Clark. The world which was still recovering from the first war can be seen inexorably moving towards the next, even in something as parochial as a British publisher's list. Meanwhile, the writers and cartoonists from the *Punch* round table did their best to make us laugh and to evoke the world of childish innocence which never was, while the eponymous *Bright Young Things* of Lewis Baumer's novel did their best to dance the night away.

Milne's refusal to go on with the Pooh honeypot might have seriously reduced Methuen's profits in the late twenties, but a new wave of enthusiasm for armchair travel carried them forward. They had, of course, published books on travel and topography since their earliest days, Sabine Baring-Gould himself being a great contributor to the genre, but the decision to approach a writer of travel pieces for the *Daily Express*, H. V. Morton, was a financial godsend. Methuen already published the 'Wanderer In' series which E. V. Lucas wrote for and may indeed have initiated. Now there was added Morton's 'In Search of' series, which was to be immensely popular and a money spinner for decades, although not on quite the phenomenal scale of Kipling and Milne.

The war had sent men and women abroad who had never

travelled before. Now, although anything more than a day trip to Margate or Blackpool might be out of the question, they could still read about the more distant and exotic parts of the globe. Morton's popularity lay not so much in the guidebook aspect of his writing, but in the description and recreation both of places that might never be visited by the reader and of those nearer home that might be reached by either hiking or biking. Following the Henry Ford principle, Morton insisted that the price of his books should be kept low, to three shillings and six pence rather than the six shillings that the firm had wanted. This made them accessible to the young clerical workers whose numbers were growing while manual jobs declined and whose legs were still strong enough to take them in search of Britain and in the steps of the master.

# FIVE

# *The Children's Hour*

## 1929–1939

A month after Algernon Methuen's death in 1924, E. V. Rieu had produced a scheme for what was to become the series Methuen's Modern Classics. Sir Algernon himself had realised the tremendous potential for the sale of schoolbooks to the rapidly expanding local authority schools but, perhaps because of his own essentially private-school background, had been unable to think of a suitable editor. Rieu had sought the opinions of an ex-chief inspector for the LCC and two other HMIs, and they had recommended J. C. Stobart, Director of Education at the BBC. He was keen on the idea, but was in the event perhaps put off by the £15 fee per volume that the company was prepared to offer, and Rieu was left to edit the series himself.

The idea was to sell at one shilling and sixpence a volume which would be an abridged version of 160 or 192 pages. The aim was to capture the market primarily as class readers for the elementary schools, and the texts were to be drawn from Methuen's own lists. Rieu assiduously sought advice, at a guinea a book, from schoolmasters and HMIs. It was the top classes of elementary schools which were the first target. J. Compton, a Manchester HMI, put it:

> The crucial age for these books is fourteen.... After fourteen boys leave elementary schools, or are concentrating on the technical side of education in central schools, or finally, in secondary schools start on their two years preparation for Matriculation etc which involves, as far as English is concerned, a detailed study of the classics and leaves little room for most of our stuff.

No mention is made of the girls, who by this time made up 50 per cent of the pupils, and the list in the beginning is heavily masculine in its interests.

Compton had been through the Methuen catalogue looking for possible titles, and his comments make interesting reading. He judged Chesterton's *Ballad of the White Horse* 'not good enough' and Belloc 'not quite good enough alone', Conrad 'too old' for fourteen-year-olds, Gilbert Parker 'a back number',

H. C. Bailey 'not quite good enough', but E. V. Lucas he welcomed warmly, which must have pleased the chairman and helped Rieu get the project through. However, others were less keen – Rieu was in the process of publishing *Open Sesame*, which was to be a very successful book of poetry for children which included a poem by non-Methuen author Edith Sitwell. Now one of his correspondents, a schoolmaster from Golders Green, suggested a prose anthology which was potentially less sexist, *Boys and Girls in Famous Books*, and which included, interestingly enough, Katherine Mansfield's *The Garden Party*, only two years after its volume publication. Sitwell and Mansfield point up between them the element which the Methuen list of this period lacked: the moderns.

Someone has annotated the proposed anthology 'very cosy'. It looks like E. V. Lucas's pencilled handwriting. The arrows to this remark in the margin run from Kipling's *Kim*, Tolstoy's *My Childhood and Boyhood*, W. H. Hudson and 'Some of Stevenson's Boys'. A further comment from Lucas says that the anthology would have to be drawn from non-copyright works and that the authors wouldn't need paying. He also doubted if young people wanted to read about young people, a view which Rieu put forward to the proposer who countered with a crisp, 'Then why do they mop up school stories? and why is Jim Hawkins the life and soul of *Treasure Island*? and why will they be swarming to see Peter Pan in a week or two? AND, why are they pestering me day after day to read them some more from *When We Were Very Young?*'

Rieu, in his reply, admitted the force of the argument but said that 'the high charge which would have to be paid for permission to reproduce' the proposed selection made it impossible. The writers, not surprisingly, wanted to be paid for this new market. 'We have had some recent and painful experiences of this sort. ...' They were anxious to include *The Wind in the Willows* in the series at a royalty of 5 per cent, whereas Kenneth Grahame felt that they should pay 10 per cent as agreed in a contract of 1921 for a school edition, and was in any case unhappy about the whole principle of abridgement.

By 1925 the series consisted of *The Wind in the Willows*, Maeterlinck's *The Blue Bird*, Jack London's *White Fang*, George Birmingham's *Spanish Gold* and a volume of stories by W. W. Jacobs. In asking advice again of J. Compton, now the Education Officer for Barking, about proposed new titles for the series, Rieu himself made some interesting comments on books which had been suggested to him. He doubted if Chesterton was good enough and hadn't read any of the four proposed titles by Conrad except *The Secret Agent*, 'for I don't like him'. The search was also on for a volume of easy plays for elementary school classroom use, but there were great problems and Rieu wrote to another of his advisers in May 1925: 'Everyone seems to want this sort of thing, but, when one sets about

THE
BLUE BIRD

By MAURICE MAETERLINCK

WHITE FANG

JACK LONDON

getting it, one meets with almost insuperable difficulties. Either the plays are slightly too sophisticated, like *The Great Adventure*, or they are obviously unsuitable, like *The Vortex*, or they are tosh!'

The next new project was an anthology of poems for children, consisting largely of A. A. Milne, Rose Fyleman and E. V. Lucas. A later editor of the schoolbooks division, Peter Wait, remembers Rose Fyleman as 'rather good. She was really quite creative, with a genuine poetic streak. She was a difficult woman, though.' He also records the antipathy between Rieu and A. A. Milne, which must have made this a hard book to put together.

By 1928 Rieu was having to look outside Methuen's backlist for new titles, but with limited success. Other publishers were, not unnaturally, eager to produce their own cheap children's editions when they realised what a success it could be. A note on sales for the first three months of 1927 shows that nearly 4,000 copies had been sold from seven titles, with *Wind In The Willows* far in the lead. Teachers were delighted with the books and the educational press produced useful encomiums for advertisement: 'This excellent series', 'among the best we have at our call', 'well printed and strongly bound', 'we have nothing but praise', 'a joy to handle'.

The smell of wet winter classrooms in the tall brick buildings, classrooms that were stepped from front to back with rigid, metal-framed all-in-one desks and forms in couples and segregated by 'boys' and 'girls', the clump of blakeyed boots on tiled stone stairways, the grubby forefingers moving along the lines of print as the chapped lips murmured the words, come off these pages, and the remembered smell of the thick paper, for they were still around when I began my schooling at the end of the thirties, and during the Second World War, dog-eared but serviceable.

Lucas had done quite well with an abridged edition of *The Gentlest Art*, a book of letters, and three Milne works had been added, including *Toad of Toad Hall*, which supplied some of the need for classroom plays, and, no doubt, relief to both beleaguered teachers and pupils when a lesson could consist of acting rather than merely reading aloud round the class. But by 1931 the familiar periodic cloud of educational cuts was dimming these bright prospects. Rieu was anxious to include one or two of H. V. Morton's travel books in the series. Morton himself was unsure whether being made into a class reader wasn't a form of literary suicide, and feared that no one would ever turn again with pleasure to something they had been forced to read in school.

He was in Edinburgh where the Scottish rep took him out for 'a rather hearty lunch' and persuaded him to let his books be published as Modern Classics. The rep, however, had his own worries about how many he would be able to sell, since:

'If the present government gets its way they will do all in their power to stop educational advance.' He was accustomed to local authorities using their supplementary readers in sets of forty-eight. 'I have a hunch that it is just this class of book that will be axed by the Authorities.' Rieu wrote calming his fears and indeed seems to have been so convinced that 'the present crisis is only temporary' that some time about now he appointed an education manager, one A. G. Barnes, who first appears in the accounts in January 1932, presumably so that Rieu himself could concentrate on developing the University series which he preferred.

There had been an attempt in 1929 to run a staff magazine, as had been done during the war years. The few remaining numbers of this first wartime effort have unfortunately vanished, but a run of twelve numbers of the thirties successor *The Gateway* still exists. The magazine folded after two years for lack of support, and it's easy to see why its heavy humour would have been hard to sustain as the thirties darkened into depression and the fanatical extremism of political left and right. There are, however, one or two interesting articles on the trade and one on Algernon Methuen himself, quoting from an earlier vanished interview.

Those articles on the trade consist of 'The Truth About Publishers' by an author, Gordon S. Maxwell, which shows how little has changed in fifty years in that edgy relationship between author and publisher, and 'The Future of Bookselling' by a bookseller which also shows that *plus ça change*. The author complains of insufficiently geared-up promotion, failure to advertise and lack of 'imagination' in seeing the potential in something unusual, citing a number of examples of later bestsellers that were turned down by several publishers: *Lorna Doone*, *The Scarlet Pimpernel*. *Sherlock Holmes* and *The Broad Highway*. Familiar swingeing stuff!

The bookseller's complaint by W. A. Cooper is familiar too. 'The habit of borrowing has increased tremendously in recent years, and chiefly through the public libraries. The original aim of public libraries was to further education and study, not to provide fiction and general literature for the masses. To think of checking this in these days of economy probably sounds absurd . . .' He goes on to castigate the publishers for their over-production of new titles and high unit costs so that the public is forced to look for cheap editions 'at every cheapjack store! It has surely reached rock bottom when Woolworths can handle new copies of recent books at sixpence each. . . . To continue with the present system means more book borrowers and stagnation for the bookseller.'

Algernon Methuen's own diktat on how to succeed in the trade was to become increasingly relevant as the firm he had founded picked its way through the difficult inter-war years.

You need to be a business man, that is to know how to buy and sell and to organise; you need to have the ability to produce a book well, and you want a certain amount of literary power ... you must have a fair acquaintance with our libraries and a love of it.... People want relief from care, they want Life presented to them in an agreeable form, they want their imagination touched, to be transported into the lives of others or to see their own lives painted by a master.

He had spoken these words in 1904 and he had kept his belief in them until at least the Great War and *The Rainbow* trial. They betray, unusually for him, a passionate trust in the power of literature to 'transport', to touch the imagination and embody life with the hand of 'a master'. Perhaps he was thinking of James and Conrad, Wells and Gissing. It was to be the fate of the firm not to attract the post-war masters, largely because, I believe, Lucas's literary taste was too well known for the agents. A study of the manuscripts submitted for 1930 contains disappointingly few surprises. Methuen failed to spot two bestsellers in their fields, John Creasey and Betty Trask, whose books were 'not accepted', and the children's writer Alison Uttley, but in literary fiction the most interesting offer was a translation of a prose piece by Luigi Pirandello, *The Bat*. The acceptances in fiction were the new Wodehouse and A. P. Herbert, but no longer the Herbert of *The Secret Battle*, though that had now reached its fifth edition with an introduction by Winston Churchill. Now it was the lightly competent touch of *The Water Gipsies* and *Tantivy Towers*, described in the new Drama section of the catalogue as a 'light opera'.

Lucas has been described as 'a man of letters', that phenomenon which no longer exists, since the various parts that made it up have largely been split under the headings of academic, journalist, writer and TV personality. The guru element, which expressed itself in yearly volumes of essays, wise and witty pieces on anything from dogs to gods, was transferred through radio to television and the newspaper columns. Lucas may, however, be said to have helped to prolong the natural life of the written essay, which in its turn seems to have been originally an offshoot of the pulpit. The desperate uncertainties of the period must have contributed to the public's need to be by turns cheered and warned by figures like Belloc, Chesterton, Lucas himself and the young J. B. Priestley, whose *Apes and Angels* Methuen also published.

It's not clear how far the new owner interested himself in the content of the books published. He didn't join the board but despatched a series of 'darts' from his mansion in Wimbledon. He seems to have been told by, among other friends in the business, his accountant E. J. G. Webb, who attended many of the directors' meetings, that the appearance of the Methuen

stock needed modernising. There's a curious note in the minutes, for example, about careful consideration being given to a suggestion of Sir George's for imitation leather bindings.

In 1932 he also seems to have been taken by a young man in the production department, Colin Summerford; he was described by Peter Wait, who became education manager in 1934 and had been at Winchester with him, as a 'clever, amusing rather feckless character' and a friend of Compton Mackenzie. Roberts began insisting that all designs for new books should pass Summerford's examination. The directors threatened to resign in a body. Their contracts were up for renewal in July 1933. To everyone's surprise, the resignations were accepted. There was a desperate attempt to patch matters up. Lucas withdrew his resignation and signed a new contract, but a fresh row broke out and the other directors stood firm. C. W. Chamberlain, the managing director; Frederick Muller, the company secretary; and Spencer Killby, head of the production department (who had all been with the company since nearly the beginning) left in a body. Lucas stayed on as chairman and literary adviser; Rieu became a director and managing director as well.

A few months later Rieu sacked A. G. Barnes, the education manager. Peter Wait was told of the vacant post by his old school acquaintance, Colin Summerford, applied and was appointed. J. Alan White, who had been with the firm since 1924, was made a director and J. W. Roberts became the company secretary. This was the group that was effectively to run the company for the next couple of years. Both Peter Wait and Alan White in their memoirs have recorded a lack of literary direction and policy, and this must in the last resort be attributed to the curiously ambiguous personality of Lucas, who was now in his mid-sixties.

Wait remembers him sitting in 'a lovely room looking out over Fountain Court in the Temple, with a chamber pot behind a screen in the corner, looking perhaps (to me at least) like a rather amiable toad, cynical, amusing and apparently idle'. Wait also points to the contrast between Lucas's mind and his writing, which was 'rather pure, associations with roses, lavender etc cropping up; in contrast to his mind which inclined to the bawdy'. This seeming idleness is also reflected in Peter Wait's feeling that there was insufficient information and control over the finances of the company. Nevertheless, there was a respectable dividend of 10 per cent in 1934 and hundreds of new titles continued to appear.

Publishing was still a slightly amateurish occupation for gentlemen and this, I'm sure, is how Lucas approached it. His chief concern was his own books, which sold in enormous quantities. Rieu, who was, by general consent, more suited to the life of an academic rather than that of managing director of a public company, must have been largely responsible for the

non-fiction side, and certainly for the very successful University texts and series like the Old English and anthropological books. Together with humour and children's books, these were to remain the list's strengths for many years.

It was perhaps the shortage of good fiction on offer through the usual channels which caused Methuen to run a competition in 1931 for 'Novels of English Life Today,' with Rose Macaulay, Gerald Gould and A. P. Herbert as the judges. Sadly, the quality of submissions was so low that the two handsome awards of £1,000 and £350 respectively to the first- and second-prize winners were unable to be given, although the judges felt that six of the entries might be published.

Peter Wait's contention that Barnes, his educational predecessor, had initiated no new titles for the Modern Classics series is borne out by the complete lack of any correspondence bearing his signature in the file. The last letter Rieu wrote is succeeded by Peter Wait's first. Clearly, although he wanted to continue with the University list, the job of managing director absorbed all Rieu's energies. However, this state wasn't to continue for long, for Rieu himself, according to Alan White's account, resigned because of the continuing hail of darts from Roberts, now Sir George in Wimbledon.

Andrew Dakers was appointed as Rieu's successor in October 1936, Rieu himself taking the translations of Homer he had been working on in his quiet moments for Penguin, which is another and well-known story and one of great success. Dakers lasted two years, at which point Lucas himself died. These management traumas could in themselves have destroyed the company, but the truth was that the whole publishing industry, along with the rest of the country, was in chronic depression. Curiously, Methuen were doing no worse than anyone else. Books continued to be published, series initiated, even profits made while others were going bankrupt. It's a tribute to Algernon Methuen's original careful building that the company managed to hang together, trading still largely on its backlist and the lines he had laid down.

It had acquired another fiction bestseller in the American writer of novels with a Chinese setting, and eventual Nobel prize-winner, Pearl Buck. Lucas himself made a trip to America, presumably in search of talent. The two-way traffic had become increasingly important, with American bestsellers boosting the fiction list and sales to the States marked up in the catalogue for spring 1933.

Alan White also introduced another, this time authentic, Chinese writer to the company in Chiang Yee, who wrote and illustrated his own 'Silent Traveller' books. Lucas continued his arrangement with *Punch* for the right to publish in book form any of their contributions, and this was the backbone of the humour list which included Bateman, Nicholas Bentley and Fougasse as well as Sellar and Yeatman's immensely successful

*1066 And All That*. In 1933 this formally became the Methuen Library of Humour under the general editorship of E. V. Knox, 'Evoe' of *Punch* and brother of Ronald, who had already been published by Methuen, principally his detective stories, but had left them for the new Catholic foundation of Sheed and Ward.

## ERRATA

P. 3.   *For* Middletoe *read* Mistletoe.
P. 9.   *For* looked 4th *read* looked forth.
P. 44.  *For* sausage *read* hostage.
        *For* Pheasant *read* Peasant, throughout.

xii

## 1066 AND ALL THAT

### CHAPTER I

#### CÆSAR INVADES BRITAIN

THE first date[1] in English History is 55 B.C. in which year Julius Cæsar (the *memorable* Roman Emperor) landed, like all other successful invaders of these islands, at Thanet. This was

Top nation

in the Olden Days, when the Romans were top nation on account of their classical education, etc.

Julius Cæsar advanced very energetically, throwing

[1] For the other date see Chapter XI, *William the Conqueror.*

Sellar and Yeatman's *1066 and All That* (1930)

In retrospect, 1933 appears a desperate year in which to launch a library of humour, but in trailering his own volume of humorous verse for boys and girls, *Cuckoo Calling*, later the same year Rieu wrote in the catalogue: 'All of us, young and old, need nonsense nowadays to keep us sane.' In the same catalogue appears Lucas's autobiography *Reading, Writing and Remembering*, and alongside it, *A History of the Nazi Movement*

translated from the German of Konrad Heiden. 'Now that it has become the dominant partner in the new National Government in Germany, National Socialism may very well exert a profound influence upon the future destinies both of Germany and Europe,' the blurb predicts. 'How did this great movement originate? What were the underlying causes of its extraordinary appeal to the youth, and not alone the youth, of Germany? Why did Hitler become its leader? These are the questions that are being asked today throughout the English-speaking world.'

It can't be alleged that Methuen as a company shirked its political duty in bringing the rise of fascism and dictatorship to the attention of the British public. The relevant titles run like a dark thread through the annual lists, beginning with the translation of Guiseppe Prezzolini's account of Italian fascism and Mussolini in 1926. The British appear to have been almost fascinated, a rabbit in the oncoming car's headlights, by what seemed this irresistible rise. Methuen inaugurated a mini-series, 'If I Were Dictator', asking public figures to say what they would do to cure the nation's and the world's ills from a position of unquestioned power.

The longing for peace, and doubt as to whether it could be maintained, are also reflected in several titles of that year: *The Science of Peace*, *The Bulwarks of Peace* and *In Pursuit of Peace*. Spain, too, was added to the causes for concern with *The New Spain* and *A History of Aragon and Catalonia*. Wait, in his memoir, graphically describes the feeling of being overshadowed by constant domestic and international crises in the run-up to the Second World War.

> At home there was severe unemployment – unmitigated by a welfare state – an economic slump, a divided 'national' government, finally a book trade burdened with over-production and poor sales. . . . These things for me at any rate coloured the whole background of life. Even in 1936 it seemed quite certain there had to be a war.

Kenneth Grahame had died in 1932. A year earlier Methuen had published the thirty-eighth edition of *The Wind in The Willows* illustrated by Ernest Shepard, whose drawings were to become the definitive illustration of *The Wind In The Willows*, as they were of the Pooh books. He was also a member of the *Punch* staff, and his version would help to keep Grahame's work both popular and in print for many years to come. The nostalgia for the lost world of the riverbank, which had surfaced in the post-war years and might perhaps have been expected to fade, was given a fresh brightness by the surrounding darkness and, like the rather frantic pursuit of the humorous, was part of the defence people assumed in order to go on living under constant threat. All these trends are mirrored in the Methuen list and make the attempt at 'Peace with Honour' more understandable.

(*opposite clockwise*)
Maurice Maeterlinck

A. A. Milne

J. B. Priestley

Luigi Pirandello

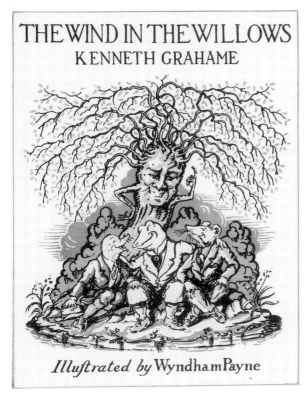

THE WIND IN THE WILLOWS
KENNETH GRAHAME

*Illuſtrated by* Wyndham Payne

Some different views of *The Wind in the Willows* by (*clockwise*) Wyndham Payne, Nancy Barnhart, Paul Branson, Nancy Barnhart; (*opposite clockwise*) E. H. Shephard, Paul Branson, Arthur Rackham, Arthur Rackham

THE WIND IN THE WILLOWS
KENNETH GRAHAME

5/- NET

METHUEN

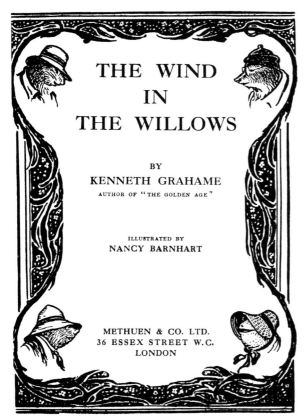

THE WIND
IN
THE WILLOWS

BY
KENNETH GRAHAME
AUTHOR OF "THE GOLDEN AGE"

ILLUSTRATED BY
NANCY BARNHART

METHUEN & CO. LTD.
36 ESSEX STREET W.C.
LONDON

THE WIND
IN THE WILLOWS

BY
KENNETH GRAHAME
AUTHOR OF "THE GOLDEN AGE"

ILLUSTRATED BY
PAUL BRANSOM

METHUEN & CO. LTD.
36 ESSEX STREET W.C.
LONDON

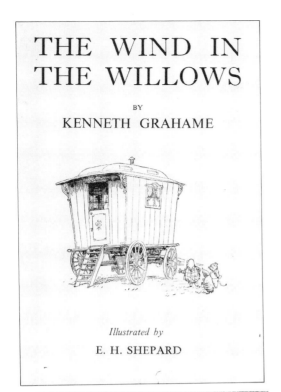

# THE WIND IN
# THE WILLOWS

### BY
### KENNETH GRAHAME

*Illustrated by*

## E. H. SHEPARD

TOAD LAY PROSTRATE IN HIS MISERY ON THE FLOOR

Rieu must have initiated the Gateway series of contemporary poets which started in 1933 with John Pudney and Randall Swingler and went on to include Humbert Wolfe and A. S. J. Tessimond, whose work was generously submitted by Pudney; this was in marked contrast to the continued outpourings of Wilhelmina Stitch, who, having taken up the mantle of John Oxenham, sold in her thousands, offering tinsel comfort with her little semi-mystical prose pieces. Young poets, always on the lookout for a new vehicle for their poetry, obviously spotted this new series and began to submit their work, but a dead hand (almost certainly that of Lucas) must have fallen over the series for in 1933, while accepting Tessimond, Methuen rejected in quick succession Rayner Heppenstall, Roy Fuller, Kathleen Nott, E. J. Scovell, Ogden Nash and John Greenleaf Whittier.

The 'strong undercurrent throughout the country for a revival of religion', noted in spring 1934, is hardly unexpected. The occasion of the remark was the first publication of *Seven Sacred Plays* by Francis Younghusband as part of the revival of religious drama in which T. S. Eliot and Christopher Fry were to play leading parts. Religion, laughter and nostalgia were the bastions against despair, helping to ensure that the British proletariat followed the road to neither left nor right. 'If I Were Dictator' made it all into a game or a set of verses for *Punch*, embodying the traditional British refusal to take ideas seriously, and to be wryly pragmatic about life in general, which in peace may be weakness, but in war becomes our strength. In 1934 A. A. Milne, an ardent pacifist, published his own or, as the public were increasingly to see it, Pooh's contribution to the great debate: *Peace With Honour*.

The religious revival itself could take strange forms as people looked around for some conviction that 'there must be more to it than this'. The occult and spiritualism became fashionable. 'It is becoming clearer than ever that psychical research is rapidly attaining the status of a science,' the catalogue announced in introducing *Inquiry Into the Unknown*, a revised series of talks given on the radio and published under the editorship of the Investigation Officer of the Society for Psychical Research. When disembodied voices could come out of a box or figures dance on a flat screen there might well be other manifestations of the unknown. The whole fashion was to be beautifully sent up by Noël Coward in 'The Stately Homes Of England':

> The stately homes of England though rather in the lurch
> Provide a lot of chances for psychical research:
> There's the ghost of a crazy younger son
> Who murdered in 1351, an extremely rowdy nun
> Who resented it, and people who come to call
> Meet her in the hall ...

(*left*) Wilhelmina Stitch

(*right*) Pearl S. Buck

Nevertheless, certain aspects of the movement had profound effects on writers like Yeats, who wanted the phantasmagoria of religion without fundamentalist belief.

At the same time Methuen continued its Westminster Commentaries, one of the series begun at the very earliest development of the list and now providing a forum for the most radical Christian thinking. For those in the thirties who still looked for a resolution within the traditional framework, there was the mystical path under the continuing guidance of Evelyn Underhill, or the resurgence of Roman Catholicism which was to sweep up Ronald Knox, G. K. Chesterton and, most importantly for literature, Grahame Greene and Evelyn Waugh. An interesting appearance is the classic work of Indian mysticism so influential in the West, *The Gita* by Sri Aurobindo, sent from his ashram in Pondicherry and introduced by the Methuen author of popular Indian stories, F. W. Bain.

These manifestations of the search for explanation and security appear alongside the pioneer work by Louis Leakey in the field of anthropology which Methuen published in 1934 as *Adam's Ancestors*, a title which raised afresh the whole question of evolution in two words, in a book based on his own field work in East Africa. Alongside the frightening political developments was the increasing pace of scientific discovery reflected in two series of monographs on philosophy and psychology which Methuen published under the editorship of G. C. Field, who held the chair of philosophy at Bristol, and in another on physics under the editorship of B. L. Worsnop of London University. The

series of physics monographs was Professor Worsnop's attempt to fill the gaps on special aspects of the subject left by the standard textbooks for undergraduates, especially his own at King's College, London and the Polytechnic. He was therefore the highly legitimate publishing descendant of Algernon Methuen himself, and the series proved as successful as Methuen's own. These series, which later extended to cover biology and chemistry, were strong enough to survive the next war.

It's easy to see now, that there were mistaken refusals of books whose authors were to become bestselling writers for other publishers: John P. Marquand and John Paddy Carstairs, Frances Parkinson Keyes and Ngaio Marsh, Nigel Balchin and Flora Thompson. There are of course always bound to be lapses of critical perception, which is why it's always worthwhile for an author to risk rejection by one publishing house after another before falling into complete despair.

In an effort, I suspect, to raise the intellectual level of the list, E. V. Rieu had taken on his sister-in-law Tegan Harris, a mysterious but influential figure, first as secretary and then as editorial assistant. Peter Wait describes her as he saw her on his arrival at the firm.

> She was a remarkable woman. She was very good-looking; rather tatty; she had long straggling grey hair and she smoked cigarettes endlessly, wearing high-necked jerseys with cigarette ash floating down. She had enormous charm, terrific energy, great critical acumen, and obviously had connections with people who put her in touch with books. I never discovered what her background was, apart from the fact that she was a great friend of L. B. Namier . . . .

As a description of a thirties bluestocking this could hardly be bettered, but the important thing is her contribution to the list and what it says about the significance of the individual editor to its development in any publishing house.

Wait goes on:

> . . . she produced for the firm novels by Malraux, Ignazio Silone and some extraordinarily good political books. . . . Not only that but she discovered Jean de Brunhoff, the inventor of Babar, and made the firm publish these delightful books, rather against their will, because they didn't think books that shape were a very good idea. For that reason *Orlando, the Marmalade Cat* was turned down, to become a bestseller elsewhere.

He appears as 'Marmaduke' in the manuscripts received ledger. Among his colleagues in non-acceptance in 1934 were

e. e. cummings's *Eimi* and a book of *Travel Sketches* by a, but not I think *the*, 'Miss Gwen John'. Ignazio Silone's powerful novel *Fontamara* was taken but not his book on *Fascism*; A. P. Herbert, Wilhelmina Stitch and Enid Blyton all had more than one book accepted that year. The friendship between E. V. Rieu and Enid Blyton, which helped to keep her contributing some of her many bestsellers to Methuen, is one of the most unlikely associations that could be predicted. She had begun as a schoolteacher publishing little stories in the *Teacher's World*, which Methuen collected, and which sold well. From this she moved on to poetry and later to children's novels. Wait remembers her as 'a model author ... always on time ... beautiful typescripts ... never argued about terms. A nice little woman ... kind, good ... a highly competent storyteller, moral, good middle-class moral standards and I think she made children want to read books.'

From very small beginnings in the eighteenth century, publishing specifically for children had become a sub-industry of its own. That story has been fully explored by others in the history of children's fiction. Methuen had made an outstanding contribution to its development from the founding of the list, which had gradually increased from one or two new titles a year to ten in 1934 when Babar made his first appearance with *The Story of Babar*, appropriately introduced by A. A. Milne, who was no doubt glad to see his mantle passed on, while his own four bestsellers appeared in a new cheap half-a-crown edition. *Babar* himself cost seven shillings and sixpence.

Methuen also announced in that year's catalogue the results of their competition for stories for children between eight and twelve years old, for which they had received over four hundred entries. The judges were Clemence Dane, E. V. Lucas and Lady Verney. The prizes were £200 for the winner, and £100 for the runner-up. There were also two new Enid Blyton collections and a radio spin-off in the form of a travel book for children based on Margaret Baumann's series for 'North Regional Children's Hour'.

The increasing influence of film and radio are reflected in the list, mainly in the form of books based on radio series which fitted into an established slot, like Gilly Potter's *Hogsnorton* broadcasts among the humour, but in 1934 the company first published a British filmscript, *The Private Life of Henry VIII*, so beginning the interaction between screen and book which is now such an important feature of the trade, with its enormous impact both on sales and literary modes themselves. The following year Methuen published the notorious *Jew Süss*, the filmscript based on the novel by Leon Feuchtwanger, edited by the film critic of the *Sunday Express*. One of the more bizarre manifestations of this new interrelationship is a first autobiographical book by the film star Mary Pickford, testifying to her faith in a personal deity which had helped her to deal with the many 'trials and tribulations' of being 'rich, successful and beautiful', and set beside this a work by Hitler's favourite filmmaker, Leni Riefenstahl.

It's hard now to recover who was responsible for initiating which series or title. There were no editorial meetings. Each editor worked independently, with whoever was managing director rubber-stamping the choices unless they were likely to be for large expensive books, when a veto might be exercised. Lucas himself, according to Peter Wait, had the final word and certainly the choices and rejections for the literary and fiction lists do have the mark of his personality. Peter Wait is unsure whether it was Jock Gibb, a fellow editor and friend, or Tegan Harris who was responsible in 1935 for a series of short books on Socialism and the Labour Party, 'Labour Shows the Way' edited by the future Prime Minister, Clement Attlee, whose blurb begins: 'The Labour Party is the alternative Government of this country'.

JEAN DE BRUNHOFF

THE STORY OF BABAR

the little elephant
with a preface by A.A. Milne

METHUEN CHILDREN'S BOOKS
LONDON

Scenario of the Film
JEW SÜSS

In parallel with this is a novel which shows that George
Orwell and Robert Tressell were not the only pre-Second World
War writers to deal with the poor from the inside: *Means Test
Man* by Walter Brierley, which describes a week in the life of
an unemployed Derbyshire miner and his family.

> A faithful picture of the moral and spiritual enervation
> which the Public Assistance system, often tactlessly
> administered, forces upon sensitive people. One-twentieth
> of the population of Great Britain live through fifty-two
> such weeks every year, and – as far as they can see at
> present – will do so till they die. It is almost the duty of
> every intelligent British man and woman to read this
> book . . . and to face up to the facts in it.

Unfortunately they seem to have been unwilling to pay seven
shillings and sixpence for doing their duty and the book sank.

In 1935 there was another attempt to produce a literary
magazine, called *Zig Zag*. 'To be published occasionally, it will
be devoted to good articles about good books and other topics
of interest to readers.' However, since the authors were mainly
drawn from the Methuen stable, the list of articles is somewhat
lacklustre. There's no mention of a cover price, so presumably
it was free to those who sent their names and addresses on a
postcard. The opening article of the first number was once
again by E. V. Lucas, on editing Charles Lamb. 1935 also saw
that bane of both publishers and authors: an expensive libel
action which involved Rieu in a trip to Belfast to defend the
company in an Irish court. The cause was the autobiography
of an ex-Irish commissioner. When asked by the judge whether
he hadn't behaved badly, Rieu replied that he thought he'd been
unlucky, which apparently amused the court and it reduced the
damages to £1,250.

Rieu had continued to develop his University series, though
relying increasingly on Peter Wait's assistance. When Rieu was
eased out in 1936, Wait continued his practice of visiting each
university for a week at a time to solicit authors, and visiting
schools to solicit sales. Meanwhile, the film books continued to
grow. *Mutiny on the Bounty* spawned *Bligh and the Bounty*,
Mary Pickford wrote a novel and her second volume of autobiography, and there was a handbook on successful film
writing. At the same time the first book on television appeared,
*Television* by A. G. D. West, to coincide with 'the beginning of a
regular high definition Television Service in London early in
1936'. It was a technical treatment of the subject, aimed principally at the 'Honours Student in Communication Science',
for whom there was as yet no other textbook.

Perhaps it was Rieu who brought in Philip Guedella, a writer
remembered particularly as a very witty man, to be literary
adviser in 1935, but he made little impression on the firm and

seems to have left in 1937. At about the same time Sir George
Roberts's accountant, Captain Webb, who also appears in the
editorial accounts, proposed that Andrew Dakers, who had
been a literary agent, should be appointed to the firm with
immediate directorial status. This dismayed the other directors.
They counter-suggested that the appointment should be on a
year's probation only and not as a director, and that it should
be made clear to Dakers that his job was in the hands of the
board. As in the case of Colin Summerford, however, Sir George
got his way. A month later the board was forced to offer him
a directorship with the weak *caveat* that they could dismiss him
at the end of a year. Sir George intervened again in April 1936
to enforce a salary for his accountant, Webb. The board agreed
to pay him when the annual dividend rose to 10 per cent.
Clearly things had been going badly and Sir George was anxious
for more profits. Dakers took his seat on the board at the May
meeting. In October Rieu resigned as director and manager and
Dakers was given his job. Rieu stayed on only as external
adviser and reader on the educational and academic side.

However, the dividend continued to sink. By 1937 it was
down to 4 per cent for the previous year and the directors were
forced to make arrangements with the bank for an overdraft
up to £2,500. By 1938 it was clear that Dakers had been
unable to satisfy Sir George's needs. Indeed, Sir George had
been speculating in property development and had lodged his
shares in Methuen with Lloyds Bank for collateral. The deal
hadn't prospered and Lloyds foreclosed. They at once nomi-
nated a new chairman, Philip Inman, virtual owner of
Chapman and Hall (which he instantly sold to Methuen) and
chairman of Charing Cross Hospital. Dakers was paid £1,200
in compensation for loss of office. L. A. G. Strong was brought
in in November 1938 as literary adviser. At the same time the
exiled C. W. Chamberlain, who had always been waiting in the
wings to make a comeback, returned to Methuen as managing
director.

E. V. Lucas had died in June and his daughter, Audrey Lucas,
produced a memoir of him. She had accompanied him on all
but one of the journeys which had produced the Wanderer
series and was his constant companion. It has to be said that
his hand on the company had been, for the last few years of
his life, stultifying rather than stimulating. He had made a
great deal of money out of Methuen as editor, author, director
and one of Sir Algernon's legatees. In return, Methuen had
profited from the sales of nearly a hundred titles, in particular
his anthology *The Open Road*, which reached forty-two editions
in Lucas's own lifetime. If the last few years of his chairmanship
had been shaky and the profits declining, the book trade as a
whole was in the doldrums. Many other firms were in a state
of collapse and Alan White, who was to become eventual head
of the firm, was able to snap up Robert Graves's Claudius

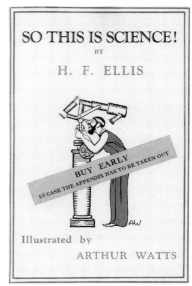

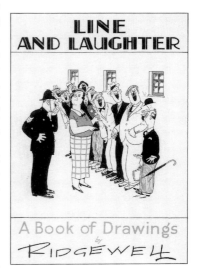

novels, *I, Claudius* and *Claudius The God* when Arthur Barker went into liquidation, as well as the bestseller *Winged Pharoah* by Joan Grant. White had previously approached Graves himself while on holiday in Majorca. He was also able to get back two more bestselling H. V. Morton titles when Rich and Cowan, to whose imprint Morton had been seduced by the disaffected Chamberlain, went bankrupt, partly as a result of paying Morton royalties rising to 33 per cent on the two books *In the Steps of the Master* and *In the Steps of St Paul*, instead of the usual top rate of 20 per cent.

The sales account for 1938 shows a turnover of £180,000 but a net profit of only £14,500. The assets, including stock and capital, were valued at just under £400,000. The new announcement lists in spring and autumn show about three hundred new titles a year, and in 1937 H. G. Wells returned to head the fiction list with *Brynhild*. The management problems of 1938 might well have thrown the firm into disarray, but a far greater cataclysm was, of course, about to overwhelm it.

The run-up to the Second World War is as unsignposted in the catalogues as that for the Great War had been. There were some, like Peter Wait, who had expected war from 1936, and others, like E. V. Rieu, who said that it wouldn't come because Hitler didn't want it. As usual, with hindsight there's the impression of fiddling while Rome burns, especially in the expanding crime fiction section, which offered relaxation from fear through simulated fear. 1938 even saw the introduction of a new category of 'Light Fiction'. In what was presumably the 'heavy' section Jack Lindsay and Norah Lofts were the two most promising and prolific newcomers.

The analysis of foreign events continued with S. H. Roberts's *The House that Hitler Built* and *Catalonia Infelix* by E. A. Peers. Dealing with home affairs, there was James Hanley's *Grey Children*, about the effects of the Depression on the mining community of South Wales, and G. D. H. Cole and Raymond Postgate's *The Common People*, which Methuen had managed to wrest from their previous publishers, Gollancz, and which became, surprisingly, a bestseller.

Yet at the same time Paul Cavanagh produced the deeply reactionary *Caesar's Wounds*, described as a 'vigorous, closely reasoned and essentially masculine book' by a 'well-known actor'. 'He is especially caustic in his comments on the neurotic exhibitionism of the emancipated woman of today', and also, incidentally, on Aldous Huxley and Noël Coward – an unlikely combination. The company incurred legal charges of seven guineas in what looks like a legal opinion on the references to Lloyd George in the book.

Even by spring 1939, when Methuen returned to the six-penny fiction market for the first time in twenty years, the political non-fiction wavered between R. W. Seton-Watson's *Munich and the Dictators* and a symposium on *The Left Heresy*

Norah Lofts

H. G. Wells

Fougasse

*in Literature and Life* in which Laura Riding, Harry Kemp, Alan Hodge and Robert Graves considered the question, 'Why so many people of apparent intelligence and good will were tempted to sink their originality and constructive ability in Left sectarianism' with special reference to the work of Auden, Day Lewis, Spender, Woolf, Mitchison, Read and Forster. There's no feeling of urgency. Titles that were planned in the spring came out as arranged in the autumn, looking uneasy against the totally changed national and international backdrop.

The new chairman, Philip Inman, wrote a foreword to a curious book by a cleric, *Masonry, Medicine and Morals*, which must have alarmed members of the staff and caused them to wonder if they had another Roberts dabbling in the company. The Fountain Library series of cheap reprints was headed by Sabine Baring-Gould, and in defiance of the times the new recruit, L. A. G. Strong, began publishing a series of one-act plays, the first titles being chiefly by himself and Rose Fyleman. They were acting texts selling for a shilling and aimed at the market in amateur theatricals which had grown up between the wars.

The most interesting new fiction in the autumn catalogue is undoubtedly Edward Hyams's *A Time to Cast Away*. Light fiction as a category has vanished but, not surprisingly, the new sixpennies were doing well. Humour continued its unrelenting publication, not yet geared up to the war effort. As the children were evacuated, gas masks issued and conscription began, it was perhaps the title of A. A. Milne's autobiography, published on 28 September 1939, which best summed it all up: *It's Too Late Now*.

I HAVE loved England, dearly and deeply,
Since that first morning, shining and pure,
The white cliffs of Dover I saw rising steeply
Out of the sea that once made her secure.

I had no thought then of husband or lover,
I was a traveller, the guest of a week;
Yet when they pointed 'the white cliffs of Dover,'
Startled I found there were tears on my cheek.

I have loved England, and still as a stranger,
Here is my home and I still am alone.
Now in her hour of trial and danger,
Only the English are really her own.

# SIX

# *Siren Song*

## 1939–1945

The immediate effect of a new war was to close the firm briefly. J. Alan White moved his family to Kent, and when the business was resumed began commuting on 'a very inadequate railway service', as he wrote to S. I. Hsiung, the Chinese dramatist whose *Lady Precious Stream*, published in 1934, had been such a success and whose *The Professor from Peking* White was in the process of publishing. Difficulties began at once with the expectation that London would be bombed, and with the immediate loss of many of the male staff to various branches of the Forces. Peter Wait and A. P. Herbert were both members of the River Emergency Service, and in great demand. Jock Gibb joined the Wiltshire Yeomanry; John Cullen, Wait's recently appointed assistant, went into the RAF. Chamberlain was by now nearly sixty-five and had been with the firm since 17 February 1896. It was impossible for him to carry it on alone, and he asked for Alan White to be given exemption from military service as the best person to help him, since although White was only thirty-five, he had himself been with Methuen since 1924. Wait, who had been able to work part-time for Methuen for the first few months, was soon called up to the RNVR.

The situation was further complicated by the chairman Philip Inman's decision in October 1940 to effectively retire from responsibility for the company for the duration of the war in order to concentrate on his other responsibility – the Charing Cross Hospital. However, the effect of this was mitigated by the addition of some of the Chapman and Hall personnel to the board. Inman had sold the company to Methuen in April 1939, and in March 1940 J. L. Bale and A. W. Gatfield made their first appearance as Methuen directors, with the immediate effect of tightening the whole financial structure of the company. Comparison month by month of figures for book production and advertising costs were made, and also on a yearly basis and between the two imprints.

The phoney war began, and after a fortnight White was able to write to S. I. Hsiung that, although they were already in trouble with some titles, business had resumed and 'Everyone seems convinced that we shall not have any very serious alarms

until Poland has been finished with.' E. V. Rieu returned as editorial adviser and to take up his old job in education for four days a week, and the quest began for a series of women to fill the empty jobs. By November the threat of paper rationing hung over the publishing industry, finally being implemented at the beginning of 1940. Firms were given an initial quota of 60 per cent of their previous year's consumption, doled out in chunks, and this shortage of paper, together with the labour problems of printers and binders, was to be the dismal theme of the forties and to largely change the whole process of publishing. Eventually Methuen's quota was 500 tons a year, a third of their pre-war needs.

The decision had to be made whether to keep old titles in print at the expense of new or to abandon the backlist in favour of fresh work. The result seems to have been a juggling between the two, although Alan White remembers that Chamberlain in particular, as might be expected, tended to favour the established titles and authors. Not surprisingly, too, the first Christmas of the war was bad for the trade in general, as Chamberlain wrote to the faithful A. A. Milne, promising him sales figures for *It's Too Late Now*. 'Business was quite good in the provinces during the Christmas season, but in London it has been particularly bad, and of course the West End has been a very great disappointment.'

Nevertheless, the book sold out its first edition of 3,000 copies and a second of 1,500. Milne, a lifelong pacifist, had voluntarily reduced his contracted advance on the autobiography from £1,000 to £375 because of the war. The firm were grateful for this and in return assured him that they intended to increase the prices of his old books. He replied through his agent Curtis Brown: 'Thank Methuens for not doing the author out of his rise in prices, as all other publishers are', presumably a reference to decreased royalty percentages. His next book of topical poems, *Behind the Lines*, originally published in *Punch* and which appeared in late 1941, was contracted for at an initial royalty of 15 per cent to 3,000, $17\frac{1}{2}$ per cent from 3,000 to 5,000 and 20% thereafter. The advance was only £200 (worth some £7,000 in terms of the 1980s).

Business had been so bad at the beginning of the war that the directors agreed to take a cut in fees along with all employees earning over £250 a year. It was hoped that these economies would be only temporary. Meanwhile, at the instigation of Chapman and Hall the question of disbanding the firm's own distribution system based in Essex Street and joining in the Book Centre scheme was investigated. Book Centre was a warehouse and distribution organisation serving several publishers. These preliminary moves were extremely cautious. Clearly the older Methuen directors were reluctant to give up a long-established part of the publishing process.

More immediately successful was the provision of an air raid

S. I. Hsiung

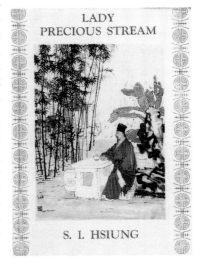

shelter for the ninety-one staff of Methuen and Geoffrey Bles, which was also shared by, among others, the staff of the local dairy and the barber's shop. Essex Street itself escaped a direct hit during the Blitz but suffered incidental damage. Chamberlain wrote to A. A. Milne on 22 October 1940, telling him that the stock of *Behind the Lines* was hung up on the railway:

> Last Wednesday morning when I reached Essex Street our offices looked like a shambles. A huge bomb had fallen at the back of the Temple and we had not a pane of glass throughout the rear of our building. All the furniture in Lucas's old room was lying about battered and broken and the whole place was in a deplorable state. For two whole days we had no water, and we are still without gas, so things are pretty miserable!

Trade was still bad. The government, in an attempt to save energy, had introduced early closing hours in the winter of 1940. Milne's book had sold just over 3,000 copies out of an initial printing of 7,500, but Chamberlain hoped that things would pick up. In an effort to improve sales, Methuen began sixpenny and shilling series of reprints. Wartime restrictions had even limited the Silent Traveller, Chiang Yee's journeyings, and he was forced to draw on memories of his visits to Yorkshire for a book 'that transports the reader out of the world of bombs and sirens into a land that is just as real but not lit with searchlights but with the light of the imagination'.

The fall of France produced several books designed to maintain her image as an ally in the minds of the British public: *The Land of St Joan* by Owen Rutter and *French War Aims* by Denis Saurat. The blurb for the second mentions 'the future of Europe in the event of an Allied victory'. So too does E. Allison Peers's analysis of *The Spanish Dilemma*, reflecting the curiously unshakeable British belief against reason and all the odds at this stage of the war that they would ultimately win.

Meanwhile the secret weapon was, as ever, humour and here Methuen's tradition and continuing links with *Punch* came into their own. Fougasse, A. P. Herbert, Cecil Hunt, Anthony Armstrong and Lionel Edwards all contributed 'to that indispensable part of the war effort which consists in cheering us all up'. Herbert himself reported that he was spending so much time on the River Emergency Service that he had 'very little time for writing of any sort'. Times were so bad that in 1940 he was asked to repay money which had been lent to him much earlier; he had been working this off in monthly instalments which had lapsed in 1932. He had disliked the idea from the beginning – 'I was always rather afraid of it' – but it had been E. V. Lucas's idea, and indeed insistence. Now his wife was having to act as his secretary. Nevertheless, he was able to produce the poems for a new collection of his light verse in 1940, *Siren Song*.

Added to the loss of sales was what seemed the burden of the government War Risks Insurance Scheme, which looked like costing the company £12,000 a year in premiums. However, as the London Blitz subsided, trade was about to pick up. Chamberlain was able to tell Milne that the sales from his five children's titles had leapt from 29,764 in the first six months of 1940 to 41,660 in the corresponding period of 1941. The problem now was to be not how to sell but how to produce, and what not to sell. Chamberlain, who was essentially a salesman and only worried by low turnover, failed to understand these changed conditions and the effect of the Government's Excess Profits Tax, which was designed to prevent wartime profiteering, and as soon as the market picked up shifted great quantities of backlist, so that by the end of the war the stock was seriously depleted. Fortunately for the firm and its employees, a scheme to top up their staff's Forces pay to the level of peacetime could be set against the Excess Profits Tax, modifying its effects and incidentally helping to ensure the loyalty of staff while they were away.

However, the combination of increased sales and paper shortage soon brought the Vintage shilling and sixpenny series to an end as prices inexorably began to rise. Some of the overseas reps had been stranded by the war and wrote home nostalgically praising the war effort, recalling the Essex Street building and sending the occasional food parcel, very welcome, especially to the ageing Chamberlain when, as Alan White noted in a letter to Chiang Yee in 1942 telling him that new Ministry of Supply restrictions meant that all illustrations must be printed back to back, 'The three winters of the war have been quite extraordinary for snow.'

White himself was exhausted by nightly Home Guard duties and felt 'I hardly have time to live'. He confirmed that 'the royalties now being paid by all publishers are much lower than before the war'. What is now the uniform 10 per cent was to be given the imprimatur of wartime conditions, from which authors have never really been able to recover it. In September 1939 Methuen had offered Robert Graves for his new novel 20 per cent to 5,000 copies, $22\frac{1}{2}$ per cent to 7,500 and 25 per cent thereafter. When he proposed a new novel on the Argonauts in August 1941, clearly expecting a similar offer, Methuen refused to pay and he was lost to the list, his determination to stick out no doubt hardened by Methuen's rejection of new editions of *Belisarius* and the poems. 'As you know we are much interested in the author but unfortunately these are not the times when we can embark on new editions of such books . . .' Cassells published the projected novel as *The Golden Fleece* in 1944.

The public demand for books, however, continued to grow. John Oxenham was brought out and dusted off for re-publication with a new selection from his First World War

poems, *Wide Horizons*, but he now had a rival in the American
writer, Alice Duer Miller's *The White Cliffs*, the verse novelette
of a First World War romance between an American girl and
a young English officer, of course of good family, who is killed
a short time after their marriage and whose son is just old
enough to fight in the Second World War. It had run through
eleven editions in America in the last quarter of 1940. Now it
rapidly notched up a sale of 40,000 copies in Britain.

> I am American bred,
> I have seen much to hate here – much to forgive,
>   But in a world where England is finished and dead,
> I do not wish to live.

It was both a pat on the back for Britain and a disguised plea
for American intervention.

A home-grown bestseller was *Behind The Spitfires* by
W. Hooper, otherwise Raff, the inventor of 'Aircraftsman Plonk',
who was himself stationed at Hornchurch. The book subscribed
7,000 copies before publication and had to be reprinted. It had
had to be approved by Hooper's commanding officer and the
War Office and was then taken up by the Sector Intelligence
Officer at Tangmere for 'propaganda purposes'.

Chiang Yee's *The Men of the Burma Road* was to be a similar
success, reprinting on publication and then going immediately
into a third edition. Yee and Hsiung were Alan White's most
industrious correspondents, Yee in particular as an artist, being
minutely concerned with the details of production and repro-
duction. Between them they exemplify a strand in British
culture which runs from Brighton Pavilion to Timothy Mo:
the fascination with the oriental and exotic which allows the
expression of a sensitivity that would be hard for an aboriginal

CHINESE PATRIOTS SING WHILE AT WORK ON THE BURMA ROAD

THE MEN OF
THE BURMA ROAD

羅鐵民

Written and Illustrated by
CHIANG YEE

METHUEN & CO. LTD. LONDON
*36 Essex Street, Strand, W.C.2*

Briton to express without seeming effete, an attitude our home-grown aesthetes had to contend with in Wilde's day, and since.

Although Essex Street itself continued to escape the Blitz, with no more than the repeated loss of its windows and main services, the destruction of a binders in 1941 caused the loss of the entire stock of Babar books which had been helping to keep up the children's spirits, along with the indefatigable Enid Blyton and a reprint of Maeterlinck's *The Blue Bird* in a special edition.

Most of the cuts in directors' salaries, including that of E. V. Rieu as literary adviser, were able to be restored in 1941. The staff had grown with the addition of more women, and improvements had to be made to the shelter. Affairs were so much better from a financial point of view that the board were able to ward off Philip Inman's attempt to buy back the profitable Chapman and Hall in 1942, and to award bonuses to Chamberlain, White and the production manager J. W. Roberts.

The difficulties of book production against this background of financial buoyancy are summarised in a letter from Alan White on, appropriately, the first of May to Christopher Grieve, otherwise Hugh Macdiarmid, whose autobiography *Lucky Poet* was in process of publication.

> Printing and binding difficulties are almost as crippling as supplies of paper.... One of the two big printers which between them formerly did the great bulk of our work was largely taken over for war production a year ago. All four of our London binders were 'blitzed' in the 1940–41 winter, and another firm in Edinburgh was burnt out by an ordinary (i.e. non-air raid) fire. In the past week we have lost our share in the work of two more small factories in Bath and Norwich.... We shall have scarcely half a dozen new books a year.

It was also taking much longer to produce a book. The average time for binding was now two months. Publishing had entered on the extended gestation period of nearly nine months per title, which has assumed almost the semblance of a natural function ever since.

Alan White's painstaking relations with the initially rather difficult Macdiarmid show the editor at his best: determined to publish a book he believed in, consulting at every stage, sympathetic to the material and the problems of creation, yet firm in pointing out the difficulties. William Gerhard, whose *God's Fifth Column* White also edited, had this to say in tribute: 'I must honestly confess that in all these years you are the first imaginatively intelligent publisher that I have yet contacted.'

The problems engendered by the war didn't, of course, in this sphere any more than elsewhere, cause all the traditional difficulties to go away. When *Lucky Poet* finally appeared in

1943, the poet Edgell Rickword sued for libel. The book had been read and reported on, and many of Macdiarmid's more swingeing comments had been modified by the author, but one at least had escaped the lawyer's eye. Edgell Rickword began by asking for the withdrawal of copies, an apology and damages. The offending passage was taken out and the sale of copies continued. In wartime conditions a whole printing was too valuable to waste. The business rumbled on for several months but eventually died away as the company refused to pay damages. A. A. Milne's *War Aims Unlimited* also had to be read as a serious possible source of libel actions but seems not to have provoked any legal cries of outrage.

Meanwhile, whatever could be published continued to be snapped up. When A. E. Coppard's volume of short stories *Ugly Anna* appeared in 1944, the whole edition was sold out on publication and there were no copies even for Coppard's local bookseller to make a window display. The problem of importing the raw materials for paper-making had been overcome. the pre-war use of esparto grass from Africa, imported in returning coal boats, had given way to the use of straw, which in the Great War had been so badly processed that thousands of books had turned black and had to be destroyed. However, techniques had improved since then. 'Almost all publishers' paper is now being made from straw and other home-made materials of which there is plenty,' White wrote to Coppard, 'but there is simply not the labour to make more of it into paper. Add to that the vast consumption of our types of paper (i.e. not woodpulp newsprint) by Government Departments and you have three parts of the story of the shortage of books.'

Coppard had been used to a pre-war flat royalty of 20 per cent. Now he had to accept $12\frac{1}{2}$ per cent to 2,000, 15 per cent above and an advance of £75, terms only a little mitigated by the complete sell-out of the eight-and-sixpenny first edition. Even the shape of books was affected as well as the quality of paper. 'How dumpy books necessarily are in wartime,' Robert Graves' agent A. P. Watt noted, while Chamberlain described the demise of the two-and-sixpenny novel to A. A. Milne: '. . . we have sold out every cheap novel up to 2/6. Unfortunately there is no possibility whatever of reprinting any of them.' Earlier in the same letter he had described the continuing boom in 'your "famous" four' which were rationed to binding 500 copies a week. 'Had we been able to get 1,000 per week of each, we could easily have sold them. For many months we have been entirely out of stock of three to four hundred titles. . . . We have had to postpone reprinting two to three hundred other books until after the war.' Even some of the supposedly dead stock from Algernon Methuen's one failure, the renamed Methuen's English Classics series, had all been sold off by the end of the war.

Here again, even before American entry into the war, there

is the conviction that all will eventually be well, a conviction not based even on propaganda but simply, perhaps, an imaginative failure to admit that Britain might conceivably lose the war, encouraged by the very British practical approach of surviving from day to day.

Even when enough copies of a book were available, they had to be released gradually on to the market to avoid lumping all the profits into one year. Printing regulations to save paper meant more words on every page, so pre-war editions all had to be re-set, with more labour difficulties, before they could be re-issued. Authors' royalties, even of the most popular writers like A. A. Milne, fell because of the smaller editions which higher prices didn't compensate for. A series of letters between Chamberlain and Milne throughout the war shows them in constant discussion of the price of each edition, another area in which the authors' involvement in the publishing process is now much less than it was. The letters also reveal, touchingly, Milne's anxious following of his son's progress through the war, which on more than one occasion made it impossible for him to concentrate on some task like producing a reader's report on a manuscript that Chamberlain had sent him for comment.

A list of new titles for which contracts had been signed, submitted by Alan White to the monthly meeting of the directors in July 1943, shows the company playing safe, maintaining its traditional tone and interests: *Ugly Anna*, short stories by A. E. Coppard; *The Battle For Britain in the Fifth Century*; *Just a Few Lines* by Fougasse and Bird; *Let's Light the Candles* by Paul Wainemann; Chiang Yee's *Silent Traveller in Oxford*; *Heather, Track & High Road*; *School German Course*; *South African Adventure*; *The Timothy Toy Trust* by Rose Fyleman and two down-market novels: *Blind Man's Buff* by Baynard Kendrick, and *Her Own Affair* by Michael Anthony.

There's nothing in this list that couldn't have been published by Algernon Methuen himself: humour, travel and topography, school texts, history, children's books and for fiction a couple of easy reads. What is lacking is anything of the weight of Conrad or Henry James. Manuscripts continued to pour in, though in decreased numbers. The ledgers had recorded over 75,000 received since they were started in 1925 to 1944. Between 1939 and the end of the war the rejections include early work by William Golding and Olivia Manning, Ronald Blythe, Edward Hyams, Josephine Tey, books by established writers including Evelyn Waugh, William Gerhardi (although he was a personal friend of Alan White), John Brophy, Wyndham Lewis, Edith Somerville and Howard Fast. Poets were particularly prone to rejection. E. V. Rieu's enterprising series The Gateway Poets had lapsed, but poets were still trying. Pudney, Tessimond, James Reeves, Charles Tomlinson, Ronald Duncan, V. de Sola Pinto and W. J. Strachan, father of a later

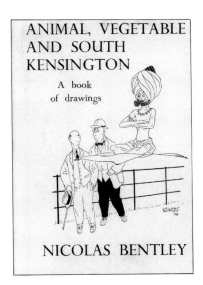

ANIMAL, VEGETABLE
AND SOUTH
KENSINGTON

A book
of drawings

NICOLAS BENTLEY

managing director, all submitted work and became casualties of the war, though several of them were published after it. Even radio favourites like Mabel Constanduros and Harry Hemsley were turned down. Two important acceptances were Isherwood's *Prater Violet* and Hesketh Pearson's *Life of Oscar Wilde*, thereby confirming the firm's forty-year association with Wilde, but both these were published late in the war.

International hostilities had for a time quieted internal rumblings but the firm's position, both as to ownership and management, remained rocky. The majority shareholding still rested with Lloyds Bank, from which Sir George Roberts, who still intervened from time to time, had been unwilling or unable to redeem it. However, the bank had made it clear to Chamberlain and White that they wished to sell as soon as a suitable purchaser could be found. The exact way in which this was done is unclear, but in December 1943 the firm was bought by Captain Nutcombe Hume of Charterhouse, not a publisher but a financier who nevertheless introduced to the board not only himself but two publishers, James Pitman and Stanley Unwin, who also bought large blocks of shares. It's possible indeed that it was Pitman, the founder of Book Centre, who had initiated the change of ownership. Pitman was also an MP and head of the Pitman firms, both publishing and printing.

The change accelerated the consideration of using Book Centre as an alternative to Methuen continuing to do their own warehousing through the printers and distribution from the offices in Essex Street, and new impetus was also given to the now lengthy discussions with Chapman and Hall on selling their premises and joining the rest of the group at Methuen, a suggestion they had been strenuously resisting. Chapman and Hall had, however, already agreed to move their distribution to Book Centre.

The new regime also called for fuller minutes and more structured board meetings, but they had bought into a very profitable organisation which could sell everything it published. The first sales report to the board on 30 March 1944 showed Methuen with a net profit for 1943 of £127,251 before Excess Profits and Schedule D Income Tax, against £73,796 for the year before.

In March the premises were hit by incendiary bombs with the loss of 30,000 educational books by fire and 5,000 novels by water, valued together at about £1,400. Milne, on receiving the news from Chamberlain, remarked that no one should be surprised since 'Hitler's dislike of education is well-known.' A survey of 36 Essex Street, carried out a few months later to comply with the War Damage Act of 1943, gives a fascinating picture of the interiors of the day which must have changed little since the twenties or even, knowing Algernon Methuen's dislike of ostentation, from the First World War. Alan White's room had green linoleum covered with a hair carpet and a blue

Oriental rug. There were long blue velvet curtains, an oak pedestal writing table, several chairs, a hatstand, an electric fire, two little tables and a bookcase; the whole lot valued, including blotter, bakelite pentray, chromium and glass smokers' tray, at £235. In the bookcase were the *Dictionary of National Biography*, the *Encyclopaedia Britannica* and other reference books to the value of £75. Chamberlain, by contrast, had a rose Turkey carpet valued at £150, an equally valuable mahogany pedestal desk, a handsome Elizabethan refectory table, several chairs, a steel filing cabinet and, among the sundries, a 'silver oxidised ape ornament', "Contemplation", valued at £2. The whole of his furniture and fittings were valued at £767 15s, but the entry mentioning two bookcases has been crossed out and there's no mention of any books. The two descriptions point up the relative positions and interests of the company's chief executives as well as reinforcing the image of Methuen's traditionalism.

In keeping with the date, the complete inventory lists blackout curtains, stirrup pumps and pails, camp bunks and bedding for fire watchers, the impedimenta of the air-raid shelters valued at £65 with only their uncomfortable-sounding deal forms for sitting on, and the 'ladies and gents enclosures', with bin, seat and lid. The gender proportions of the staff had been completely reversed by the war. There had been a ratio of roughly ten women to eighty men at the beginning of the war, which had become the exact opposite by the end, with a subsequent turnabout in lavatory provision, which was always to be a headache for Alan White. There were twenty-three typewriters in use valued at £850, and the complete stock was valued at just under £21,000, including the telephone switchboard and the electrical fittings.

The inventory also gives a precise breakdown of the departments: stock; the machine room with duplicators; the cashier's department; Miss Redman's publicity; binding; illustrations; education; jackets (Mr Walton); paper; production (Mr Taylor); the general office with the trade counter, also known as the 'Town' department; the 'Country' department, presumably for the use of visiting reps; accounts; and the extensive packing department. The physical business of production and distribution thus took up the major part of the premises, with the editorial staff squeezed mainly into Alan White's room and the education department.

The substantial Excess Profits Tax, which the company had to pay because of Chamberlain's insatiable addiction to selling books, caused the new board a grave headache, and the minutes show them twisting and turning in their negotiations with the Tax Inspector in an effort to reduce it, even though sales were down in 1944. One of the Chapman and Hall directors thought that any publicity given to 'the large though fictitious profits would make authors dissatisfied with their

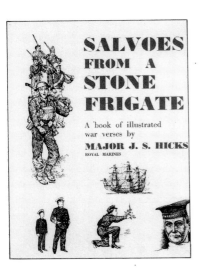

royalties'. On one occasion only, the terms for all the books bought since the previous two-monthly meeting actually appear in the minutes. They show that Pearl Buck, for instance, was paid a flat royalty of 25 per cent against an advance of £1,000, that children's books usually began at 10 per cent, that the top mystery writer Cecil Freeman Gregg began with a low advance of £100 but on a royalty of 15 per cent, that general or educational non-fiction books like *British Imperial Policy in the Twentieth Century* by J. L. Morrison, published at fifteen shillings, had a low advance of £50, but began at $12\frac{1}{2}$ per cent. Many seem to have been written by academics who could afford to wait for their return.

The 1944 spring list of new books was small, and Chamberlain explained that this was because of the policy of keeping backlist books alive. The new directors supported this, but in retrospect this decision has been questioned. It wasn't a universal policy among publishers and Alan White later felt that Methuen, in supporting their established authors, missed new talent which others were quick to snap up. Nevertheless, the old favourites were wanted by the public and were profitable, and from the writer's point of view it would have seemed particularly hard after years of loyalty to a publisher to be dropped in favour of new writers, while one's backlist was being rapidly sold off at a lower price. By 1945 the catalogue, which had numbered 4–5,000 titles in print in 1940, now numbered only 1,500.

This war produced no equivalent of *The Secret Battle* in Methuen's list, but one of its publications was to become a classic in another medium which couldn't, I'm sure, have been foreseen at its publication. It was an anonymous diary costing only five shillings: 'the intimate, human story of the life of a London AFS man who joined the Fire Service on the outbreak of war . . .' It was *The Bells Go Down*, which was to be arguably one of the most famous British films of war or peacetime.

Dorothy L. Sayers, who was a friend of E. V. Rieu and, although Gollancz published her detective stories, must have realised that he was unlikely to take on her religious writings, had initiated, as an outside editor, a new series called Bridgeheads, which was clearly a response to a mood of serious reconsideration of ethical and social values, and which made one of the periodical attempts to re-establish the importance of the imagination in human life. It's not clear how well the series did, but the growing problems of production as the war dragged on may have caused it to be abandoned in favour of disconnected pamphlets on social and philosophical themes by Sayers herself, like *Why Work?*

A series which did, perhaps most surprisingly, survive was the Twickenham Pope, a companion to the Arden Shakespeare, although in common with other titles its latest addition was likely to be delayed and passed on from one announcement

catalogue to the next. Nevertheless it had reached volume five, *The Dunciad*, by the end of 1943. The seasonal lists were becoming thinner and thinner as the backlog of production built up, even though minds were already turning to 'after the war'. Chiang Yee wrote to Alan White from Oxford in June 1944: 'There have been some great news lately. Let's hope to see the end of the war on [sic] this part of the world soon.'

The output of humour continued throughout the war. A. P. Herbert in particular contributed poems to magazines which Methuen collected into a series of books which trace the course of the war: *Siren Song*, *Let Us Be Glum*, *Bring Back The Bells*, *Less Nonsense*, and *Light the Lights* are a remarkable commentary on British attitudes during these years, a mixture of cynicism and patriotism, common sense and sentimentality, that contributed greatly to the ability to survive the psychological and physical pressures of five years of war.

> I wish I knew – I wish I knew
> (So many people seem to know)
> Exactly what we ought to do
> In order to defeat the foe.

As 1945 began, former employees wrote to enquire about their chances of reinstatement. Alan White's first response was to suggest that a circular be sent to all those staff in the Forces offering them their old jobs back at pre-war salaries, plus any increase the board thought they might have been given had the war not intervened, but this generous and obviously correct proposal was crushed by Captain Nutcombe Hume, who maintained that it would be a mistake to issue any general statement and that each individual solicitation should be dealt with separately. 'Such applicants could be told frankly whether their prospects of permanent employment were good or bad.'

As the minutes rather quaintly put it, the return of male employees 'necessitated dispensing with the services of a number of young women who have been of considerable help in the war years.' It was hoped that Stanley Unwin and James Pitman might be able to employ some of them in their expanding new businesses and they both agreed to look into the possibilities. The girls had, in some cases, been sent from the Ministry of Labour in batches of half a dozen and many of them had only lasted a week. Conditions at Methuen were still Victorian in many ways. Surnames were always used, though the girls used first names among themselves. Saturday morning working had had to be abandoned because of transport difficulties. At Christmas, instead of working until the very last minute, some of the girls went out for a drink at lunchtime and came back rather giggly, to be reprimanded by an outraged Chamberlain and an unwilling White.

On the day the war in Europe ended in May 1945, Chamberlain suffered a severe stroke and was in hospital for several months. At his instigation White became acting managing director. Chamberlain recovered slowly, still hoping to return to the firm, but in January 1946 he was forced to admit that this was beyond him. He wrote to Curtis Brown on his retirement as managing director of his 'long innings' and his intention to remain as chairman. 'I shall be "not out"; . . . and shall attend regularly though less frequently at the office.' He commended White to them: 'I cannot help thinking of him still as a young man, but that is a foible of my own advancing years. Actually he has been with the firm for over twenty years . . . I should like to commend him – which is to say commend the firm to Methuen to your continued favourable consideration.'

Inevitably, there's an end-of-an-era element in his going; the last real link between founder and firm was being broken, and something new had to be made. At the end of July Chamberlain's illness forced him to give up the chairmanship too, and he died two months later. In his letter of resignation to the board he shows the depth and root of his attachment to the firm: '. . . may God bless this wonderful Business whose care was passed on to me by the Founder . . .' Alan White's *Bookseller* obituary attributed his death to the strains of the war years: 'with the shortage of staff caused by the call-up, he stayed longer hours than ever and was to be found at his desk sometimes on Saturday afternoons and even on Sundays.'

Seven of Chamberlain's years with the firm were among the most successful in its history. White again: 'He was an admirable manager with a clear grasp of fundamentals and an absolute faith, which he never abandoned, that he could not go wrong if he followed the traditions of the founder. His determination and business sense carried him to success.' Even though he rarely read a book, he still dealt personally with the company's longest-established writers like Herbert and Milne.

The chairmanship was now vacant. Chamberlain would be a hard act to follow, but it seemed that several of the directors would like to try.

Memorial plaque to
C. W. Chamberlain

# SEVEN

# *Existentialism &*
# *Academe*
### 1946–1959

In the event, by a process of behind-the-scenes juggling and combination, the oddly named banker H. Nutcombe Hume emerged as the new chairman, a man with little publishing experience, unlike the other possible contenders, Pitman and Unwin, but with a shrewd financial head and useful contacts. His appointment left Alan White free as managing director to run his own business of publishing and to rebuild his team. Peter Wait, who had returned from the war along with John Cullen to be one of Alan White's chief editorial assistants, though not yet then a director, remembers Hume as a 'wonderful father figure'.

> I remember once when things seemed to be going badly and Alan White said: 'God, what are we going to do about our overdraft?' And Hume answered, 'Well, you go to your bank manager and say I want a bigger overdraft. And if you don't get a bigger overdraft you just kick him downstairs and go to another banker.' That's the sort of man he was. He was splendid!

The first job was to build up the stock and increase production, but there were still shortages of both paper and skilled labour, as well as the threat of a post-war slump as Lend–Lease was ended abruptly by the Americans, and a virtually bankrupt Britain tried both to establish a welfare state and to eradicate the worst effects of endemic poverty, while converting its economy from war to peace in a changed world where it could no longer take its traditional markets for granted. It was to take at least two years before the paper stocks approached the pre-war level.

The shortage of newsprint led to many printing operatives looking for jobs in book publishing on their return from the forces, but even when sheets could be printed there was still a serious shortage of binders. Nevertheless, Alan White was anxious to build up the list, especially on the educational side, as it had become clear in the last eighteen months of the war that Britain was at last to set about truly 'educating our masters'. Distribution was particularly nightmarish, with

BRITAIN
IN
PEACE AND WAR

*drawn by*
FELIKS TOPOLSKI

*with an introduction by*
JAMES LAVER

METHUEN & CO. LTD.
LONDON
1946

bombed premises and a continuing petrol shortage. The books were housed in a large warehouse at Tottenham and in Joe Davis's ex-billiard saloon. Horse-drawn vans shuttled between these and the Essex Street offices 'feeding in stock hand to mouth'.

The answer now clearly seemed to be to join in the Book Centre venture at Neasden and the agreement for this was made in 1946 to take effect from the beginning of 1947. This left more space in Essex Street and Chapman and Hall were reluctantly forced to move into co-habitation with Methuen, reinforcing the identify of the emergent group.

In keeping with the boom in education, Methuen began a Home Study Series edited by B. Ifor Evans, a kind of forerunner of the Open University. The books ranged from *A New Entry to Chemistry* through literary criticism, history and politics to *How To Run a Small Farm*, and it was described as:

a series dedicated to the reconstruction of thought and study in this post-war period. For the six years of the war, important investigations in the sciences have been proceeding, but hundreds of thousands of men and women have been deprived of opportunities of following their development. Similarly, there have been new approaches and conclusions in the study of economics,

history and literature and other branches of knowledge. In this series it is designed to construct a library in which this knowledge of the modern world can be made readily available.

The first truly post-war announcement list for spring 1946 has seventy new titles, but several of these were to continue to appear as forthcoming in subsequent lists. Fiction heads the categories again with a new Pearl Buck and a novel by the loyal and indefatigable A. A. Milne, *Chloe Marr*. War still figures in John Lodwick's *Myrmyda*, about a Commando raid on a Greek island, and Olaf Stapledon's 'fantasy', *Death Into Life*, the story of the rear gunner of a bomber who is killed along with the rest of the plane's crew. The significant title is Christopher Isherwood's *Prater Violet*. Isherwood has described his defection from the Hogarth Press to join, eventually, the Methuen list, in *Christopher and His Kind*, which Methuen published in 1977. He writes:

> ... Christopher was suffering from pique. Although *Mr Norris* had been well reviewed and had sold well, Virginia Woolf hadn't invited him to meet her. Therefore, when other publishers approached him with offers, he had entered into an informal agreement with Methuen, the highest bidder. It was understood that they were to become his publishers as soon as he could get free from the Hogarth Press.

However, it wasn't until an extremely fruitful post-war visit to America by Alan White that Isherwood's move to Methuen was finalised several books later. They were to go on to publish among others *Down There on a Visit*, *The World in the Evening*, *The Condor and the Cows* and *A Single Man* during the remaining four decades of Isherwood's life.

The firm's connection with Einstein, begun so long before by Algernon Methuen, was maintained in a new edition of *The Meaning of Relativity*, updated by Einstein with an appendix discussing certain advances in the theory since 1921. Einstein had written to Alan White, leading him to suppose that he had a whole new book to offer Methuen. White went over to the United States and on a sweltering summer day visited Einstein at Princeton, where he was disappointed to be given only half a dozen sheets of paper covered with figures. On seeing his dismay, Einstein, whom White remembers wearing a thick jumper in spite of the heat, suggested that they should be added to a new edition of an older work. 'I was never a writer,' he is reported to have said, 'my friends always helped me out.' White returned with his six pages, added them on as suggested, and printed a daring 20,000 copies, all of which sold out. Methuen also kept up and extended their archaeological list with important new books on *Dating the Past* by Frederick E. Zeuner and V. Gordon Childe on *Scotland Before the Scots*.

There is something strange in seeing one's own education and intellectual development catalogued systematically in a particular publisher's output. Turning the pages of Methuen's lists for the late forties and fifties I can almost smell the books and the surroundings in which I first encountered them. In 1951, for example, I was attending evening classes at Goldsmith's College while waiting to go to university after taking the new 'A' level examination. My tutor for English was P. J. Stead, whose *Songs of Restoration Theatre* Methuen published in 1948, and in which I had my first encounter with the name Aphra Behn, which was to lodge in my unconscious until it emerged twenty years later in a biography.

Two more of Methuen's publications had a formative influence on me as I swung, like so many others of my generation who had been children during the war, between mystical Christianity and existential humanism: Evelyn Underhill's *Concerning the Inner Life and the Progress of the Soul* (1947), and Jean-Paul Sartre's *Existentialism and Humanism* (1948). It was perhaps the last time that books would have such a profound effect in developing and reflecting the ethos of a period, the last flowering of an exclusively literary culture before the serious intervention of television and other communication technologies. Underhill had appeared in Methuen lists before the war. Her work was reissued now as the Anglican counterpart to the reinvigorated intellectual Roman Catholicism of writers like Graham Greene, Georges Bernanos, Charles Péguy and Henri de Montherlant. Together with Eliot and Fry, she helped maintain that peculiarly English version of the spiritual life that has its roots in Walter Hilton and Julian of Norwich.

A perhaps surprising addition to the religious debate was A. A. Milne's long poem 'The Norman Church', published in 1948, with its radical (for those days) suggestion that it is only male dominance that has accustomed us to think of 'God' as "Him".

> Had women ruled, we should refer
> To our imagined God as 'Her';
> And build upon the sex implied
> A Mother-legend to provide
> A creed for all, as much, as little justified.

The 'new approaches to history and literature' which the catalogue noted in its introduction of the Home Study Series as having been inaccessible because of the war, were largely continental, and their inclusion in the Methuen list reflects Alan White's own tastes and interests. These were implemented by John Cullen and by Halfdan Lynner, a Norwegian who had come to England in 1948 to look for a job in publishing and

whom White had engaged first as assistant production manager. After a year he was appointed export manager, and after the retirement of J. Roberts, one of Methuen's oldest staff, in the 1950s, sales manager. In this capacity he travelled not only Britain but Europe, selling mainly the academic book list and coming back with books and offers of new series.

At this time books that had been rejected earlier now reappeared, like W. J. Strachan's *Apollinaire to Aragon* which John Cullen published in 1948. It was probably also through John Cullen's interest in France (his wife was French) that Sartre came to the Methuen list. Sartre's version of existentialism was not popular in England, where it was in conflict with the home-grown logical positivism, which had greater appeal with its pragmatic no-nonsense British philistinism. Methuen also published Sartre's *What Is Literature?* In the Bridgehead Series, edited by Dorothy L. Sayers, the Christians fought back with Helmut Kuhn's *Encounter with Nothingness*, a rejection of existentialism, but to many of us who were young at the time, existentialism, with its doctrine of self-conscious individual responsibility and constant choice seemed not 'nothingness', but creative and energising freedom, coupled with the taking control of our own lives and actions.

The continental emphasis of the list included Christopher Fry's translations of Anouilh's *Ring Round the Moon* and Giraudoux's *Tiger at the Gates*, André Malraux's *La Condition Humaine* which appeared as *Man's Estate* in 1948, and Antonia White's translation of Marguerite Duras's *A Sea of Troubles* in 1953, all stemming from John Cullen's twin interests in the theatre and European culture.

Britain's rapidly expanding university programme with, in particular, its increasing number of places for women, demanded new academic titles. The enlargement in the number of English departments alone and their intake is variously reflected in the new series which begin to appear in the catalogues. Methuen's Old English Library, begun in 1950, was a staple of my own three-year stint of Anglo-Saxon, while the growing interest in American literature and its appearance on syllabuses as an 'option' is reflected in the American Men of Letters Series which Methuen began in 1949, bought in from America where it was run by an editorial board of Joseph Wood Krutch, Mark Van Doren, Lionel Trilling and Margaret Marshall. In 1951 James Berryman himself produced the volume on Stephen Crane.

The Twickenham Pope, which had so surprisingly survived the war, was continued and the series was completed after a suspension of six years, along with a complete reprint of the plays of Christopher Marlowe. The major task that had to be undertaken on the academic front, at the instigation of B. Ifor Evans, was a reappraisal of the Arden Shakespeare, some of whose volumes had been in print for half a century and were

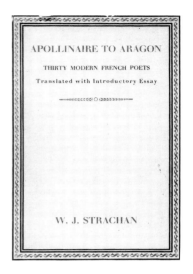

APOLLINAIRE TO ARAGON

THIRTY MODERN FRENCH POETS

Translated with Introductory Essay

W. J. STRACHAN

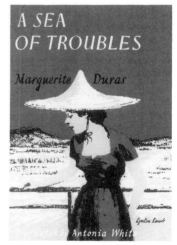

A SEA
OF TROUBLES

*Marguerite Duras*

*Antonia White*

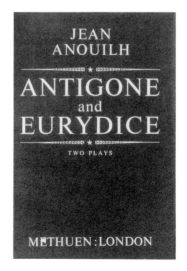

JEAN
ANOUILH

ANTIGONE
and
EURYDICE

TWO PLAYS

METHUEN:LONDON

(*clockwise*) Jean Anouilh

André Malraux

Jean Giraudoux and Louis Jouvet

still selling well. On this Una Ellis-Fermor was asked for her advice and produced a brilliantly comprehensive report on every volume that showed that nothing less than a new Arden was needed, which she was asked to edit. The series was announced in 1950 with the first volume, *Macbeth*, edited by Kenneth Muir. Meanwhile, G. Wilson Knight had expanded his interpretation of Shakespearian tragedy, *The Wheel of Fire*. Shakespeare industry was under way, although the British contribution was soon to be overtaken by the acres of Shakespeare criticism spawned by American academic institutions. There were other new studies in English literature and language which became the standard works for my generation: T. R. Henn's book on W. B. Yeats, *The Lonely Tower*; C. B. Wrenn's *The English Language* and Richard Church's *Growth of the English Novel*, among them.

The price of books was beginning to rise; by 1949 the lead novel, Pearl Buck's *The Bondmaid*, cost twelve shillings and sixpence and Hesketh Pearson's new biography of Dickens was eighteen shillings. There were, however, one-shilling-and-sixpenny Guild paperbacks of A. P. Herbert, Conrad and others and a series of hardback reprints of 'famous' novels still at the old price of six shillings, which included Wells, Bennett, Conrad, W. W. Jacobs and Pearl Buck. Methuen's profits continued to increase, but this was due at first to rebates on the Excess Profits Tax. In September 1947 the company arranged for an overdraft facility of £70,000. Nevertheless, in July of that year it was decided to buy a substantial share in the Foster Bookbinding Company.

Realising that he was unlikely now ever to become chairman, Sir Stanley Unwin resigned from the boards of both Methuen and Chapman and Hall in the middle of 1947. The team now consisted of the banker Nutcombe Hume as chairman, Alan White as managing director, with the editorial assistance of Peter Wait and John Cullen, who were made directors, and L. A. G. Strong as chief literary adviser. E. V. Rieu also seems to have renewed his connection with the firm, which published his *Iliad* and *Odyssey* in handsome hardback editions. Strong's novels were also being systematically reprinted.

Unfortunately, the fiction list had been neglected because of the deliberate decision to pursue a strong academic line. It is argued by Alan White and Peter Wait that Methuen had always had an important educational side and that Algernon Methuen had underlined this by his appointment of E. V. Rieu shortly before his death. The sciences too were developed with the first two important monograph series, and it was after all Methuen himself who had 'discovered' Einstein. Nevertheless, in his day the firm had published both fiction bestsellers and quality fiction, and it is the writers of fiction whose names are remembered, whether Corelli or Conrad. Academic works are important for their generation, but they are of their nature obsolescent

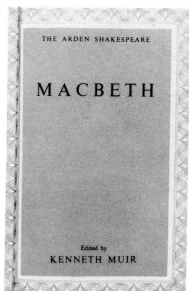

THE ARDEN SHAKESPEARE

MACBETH

Edited by
KENNETH MUIR

as soon as they are published, although the process may be drawn out, as in the case of the first Arden series over half a century. Very much of the time, though, fiction has the potential for immortality. Non-fiction can provide the economic return, the steady sales until the book is superseded by a new discovery or a change in academic fashion, as Richard Ellman's biography of Oscar Wilde has overtaken Hesketh Pearson's which Methuen published in 1946, and H. Montgomery Hyde's which they published in 1977.

The firm also maintained its connection with Wilde in a new edition of his essays edited by Pearson, and a complete version of *De Profundis* with an introduction by Wilde's son Vyvyan Holland, though Alan White decided against an edition of Wilde's letters in 1952 after five months of deliberation. As its chief fiction name Methuen had Wyndham Lewis, whose earlier works they began reprinting after the war and whose *Human Age* trilogy they also published. Alan White had orginally met him as a young man through his interest in Lewis's paintings. Lewis's reputation has always been ambiguous in Britain because of his rather Poundian political stance, and perhaps too because we find it hard to take seriously anyone so obviously talented both in literature and painting. White certainly believed in him as a creator of important fiction and not only published his own work, but commissioned an important study of him by Geoffrey Grigson and a full-blown critical biography by Hugh Kenner, who remains an admirer of his work to this day.

The *Little Reviews Anthology* of 1949, edited by Denys Val Baker, points up what was otherwise missing from the Methuen list. The contributors included many of the names which are still remembered from the creative literature of the forties and fifties, including Dylan Thomas, V. S. Pritchett, David Gascoyne, Pamela Hansford Johnson, John Heath Stubbs and so on, names that don't otherwise appear in the Methuen catalogue.

The board itself discussed how 'bestsellers' were to be found. But apart from Pearl Buck, Methuen had to rely heavily on their backlist, particularly H. V. Morton and children's classics by Milne and Grahame, for these. August 1951 saw the publication at last of *The Wind in the Willows* with the illustrations that Grahame had always wanted by Arthur Rackham, but by then E. H. Shepard's had become the definitive images of Toad and Rat and Mole, as they were for Christopher Robin and company. Enid Blyton continued to dominate the children's list (in spite of being disliked by Methuen's part-time children's editor Eleanor Graham), with title succeeding title of both stories and non-fiction and against the opposition of many parents, teachers and librarians. Children loved her books. They provided easy-to-read adventure that in its simplicity of style prefigures television and radio soap operas, with their constantly changing situations and limited vocabulary.

The war had been a good time for sales, but by 1949 the book trade was going through one of its periodic crises, painfully delineated by Michael Joseph in his complacently revealing *The Adventure of Publishing* in the late forties. Money was now tight after the spendthrift days of the war, and there were still shortages of the basic publishing needs: paper, skilled labour, and new goods and services to compete for the public's scarcer shillings in what J. B. Priestley called, and Joseph quoted approvingly, 'the transition from a war-time to a peace-time economy and production in a half-ruined world'.

Joseph's proposals were: the maintenance of paper control to keep down production; that the Publishers Association should act like a medieval guild to restrict entry to the trade; that publishers should restrict the number of titles; that houses should combine for cheaper administration; that publishers should agree an advertising cutback and abolish remainder and ex-library sales; that there should be a charge for borrowing at public libraries and that the commercial library charges should be increased; that books should be made attractive to the public with promotional fairs, book weeks and exhibitions; that the BBC should be persuaded to give tax incentives and official support to developing overseas markets; that publishers should co-operate to stop the production of dozens of titles on the same subject.

Forty years later few of these recommendations have been put into effect, though several of them have been tried, however briefly. Joseph admitted to liking publishing because he did not think that 'publishing is hard work. If it is I have never noticed it. I like publishing because it is possible to survive one's mistakes... When I read *Tess of the D'Urbervilles* and *Villette* I know I should have turned down Hardy's novel and insisted on drastic alterations which Charlotte Brontë would have indignantly rejected.'

One at least of his suggestions was taken up by the Publishers Association, which set up a working committee to examine what was seen by Michael Joseph and others as an excessive use of, and competition for, advertising. Publishers were required to sign an undertaking, presumably to limit its use, which the board of Methuen complied with at a meeting in March 1948.

Chamberlain's policy of selling as much as possible during the war had left stocks very depleted by pre-war standards, and every effort was made to remedy this. New titles were commissioned and the backlist was reprinted. However, reading habits had changed, and were to change even faster. The board noticed a resistance to new authors and earnestly discussed whether they were justified in risk to the company of taking them on. As managing director, Alan White argued strongly that it was a justified risk if there were to be any future bestsellers and a backlist. Nevertheless, he was forced to limit his risk-taking, especially in new fiction. The board minutes

1956

show greater reliance on an increasing overdraft, which at one point reached £125,000. Fears of shortage led to an over-stocking of paper which was nevertheless consumed by cyclical paper shortages, largely due to political decisions by foreign, principally Scandinavian, governments.

The high stocks of paper and unsold books by 1952 showed up as a low turnover, liquidity and profits. It was decided that manuscripts should continue to be bought, but their production would be postponed to avoid too much dead stock. The board's minutes show them wrestling throughout the late forties and early fifties with problems of cash and production flow in the face of 'national buyer resistance'. Meanwhile, the Book Centre venture, which it had been hoped would cut distribution and warehousing costs and increase efficiency, wasn't working out as planned and became an increasingly heavy burden.

There were paper and printing difficulties in 1950 and the public resisted the higher prices that necessary wage increases made inevitable. In 1951 a complete financial reconstruction of Book Centre became necessary, and the board, having inves-tigated the possibility of setting up their own distribution again, concluded regretfully that they would have to continue to support Book Centre. All publishers were feeling the pinch. In 1950 Methuen were approached about the future of Hutch-inson. They had already taken over the educational list of the Pilot Press, together with its editor Patrick Thornhill, a year before for what now seems a very modest price of £3,050. Now Batsford withdrew from partnership in the long-running Little Guides series. In January 1955 an anonymous buyer showed an interest in the company and the board was interested in its turn.

It isn't clear if this was indeed Eyre and Spottiswoode, who began to make serious moves towards amalgamation in May 1956. At the same time Alan White received an approach from George Weidenfeld to acquire his firm of Weidenfeld and Nicol-son, but the board wasn't interested in it 'as a going concern', though they thought 'it might be possible at a later date to offer Mr Weidenfeld an engagement with the company if he divested himself of Weidenfeld and Nicolson'. It's tempting to speculate on how that would have changed publishing's history.

A trip by Peter Wait to Canada and the USA had led to what seemed at first an encouraging link-up for Methuen with John Wiley and Sons, the scientific publishers, who were selling agents for Chapman and Hall in the USA. Methuen saw this as a chance to be less cautious in their production at least of scientific books, and sold some individual titles to Wiley. But in the event Wileys decided to go it alone and set up their own European distribution, thus depriving Chapman and Hall of an estimated £150,000 of trade a year in Wileys' books (for whom they had been the European distributor), to the detriment of the whole group.

138

Fiction was still languishing, and the board was quick to spot the deadly impact of television, which had really come into its own with the televised coronation of 1953. Now everyone aspired to a set, and when E. J. Taylor completed his fifty years of service with the company in 1953, that was what he requested as his 'suitable token to mark the occasion'. Aware of this deficiency, the board decided to try to strengthen the fiction list, and this policy appeared to be borne out by the appearance of condensed books and digests which seemed to promise an extended life to novels 'of entertainment value'.

By now, however, the firm's chief reputation was for educational, scientific and non-fiction books, with a strong children's list, and Thelwell and David Langdon maintaining the old connection with *Punch* and humour. Thelwell's first book for Methuen, *Angels on Horseback*, was published in 1957 at the instigation of Frank Herrmann, the Production Manager. It isn't easy to regain an area once given up. Authors and agents tended not to submit work that seemed inappropriate to the lists and the manuscript registers show a heavy weighting of submissions towards non-fiction.

This wasn't, however, the only factor at work. The emphasis on English literature itself isn't constant: it swings periodically from fiction to drama or poetry or, as now, to film. The late forties and fifties was the time for such a swing to drama: Eliot, Fry, Anouilh, Giraudoux and Sartre at first, and then the new wave, signalled in the Methuen lists by Brendan Behan's *The Quare Fellow* in spring 1957. The 1956 production of John Osborne's *Look Back in Anger* at the Royal Court Theatre heralded the beginning of this second wave, which was to be urged along by Kenneth Tynan's hot-from-the-stalls critical appraisals. The theatre was suddenly a place of great excitement again as Joan Littlewood's Theatre Workshop at the other 'Royal' in Stratford East added its own innovative productions to the rapidly developing English stage in a sudden explosion of creative talent among writers, composers, directors and designers.

John Cullen, with his own deep interest in the theatre, was quick to seize on this new development, which was to become the Methuen Modern Plays series. At the same time Peter Wait initiated The Revels Series, reprints of Shakespeare's contemporaries which began the following year.

The interest in drama was undoubtedly encouraged by L. A. G. Strong's presence in the firm and on the board, which ended only with his unexpected death after an operation for a hernia in August 1958. As a tribute, Methuen published his autobiography *Green Memory* the following spring. His many literary and theatrical contacts had helped to sustain the firm's literary side against the pull of non-fiction. Brendan Behan's *The Hostage*, published in 1958, was followed the next year by Shelagh Delaney's *A Taste of Honey*, the first play to be published

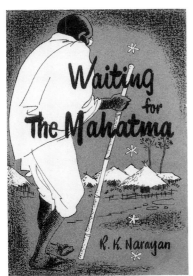

as a paperback original, and the Modern Plays series was well launched.

Almost, it seems, by accident, Methuen had managed to acquire a modern fiction classic in R. K. Narayan, whose *Waiting for the Mahatma* they published in 1955, though another classic-to-be with the same initial, Nabokov, was rejected. They had bought several of Narayan's early titles in 1951, but overstocking had delayed their production. As the fifties progressed, the increasing difficulties of managing the overall affairs of the group withdrew Alan White from the editorial and creative side of publishing into the financial and managerial side although he continued to deal with older authors like A. P. Herbert, and personal contacts like Hesketh Pearson in whom the firm had an indefatigable biographer of Wilde, Whistler, and Shaw. He also kept up a laborious correspondence with Edith Somerville until her death. By the mid-fifties he found it increasingly difficult to provide this kind of authorial support, and the story goes that the company almost lost H. V. Morton who, living abroad, began to feel subject to epistolary neglect.

What books should be published were discussed at a weekly editorial meeting on Wednesdays, which usually lasted an hour and a half to two hours. There was complete freedom for Peter Wait as head of the academic side and John Cullen on the general list to make their own free choices both of individual books and overall development, and this freedom with its concomitant responsibility they also encouraged in their assistants. Methuen were by the end of this period producing over two hundred and fifty new titles a year, including new editions and reprints. In both the academic and educational worlds they were among the leaders and immensely respected. It says much for Alan White's management that he was one of the first publishers to send a sales manager out to actively promote the books in schools and colleges, and around the world. Halfdan Lynner was instrumental with John Cullen in securing Bertolt Brecht for Methuen, visiting Brecht's widow and German publisher in Berlin to sort out the very complicated position of the copyright. Cullen was assisted by his English translator John Willett, who also helped to launch the *Tintin* series of children's books, which from a gamble exploded almost overnight into a long-running bestseller. Eleanor Graham left Methuen to become Penguin children's editor. She was succeeded by Leila Berg, also on a part-time basis and herself a distinguished children's writer, and finally by Olive Jones, the first full-timer. The children's list leant heavily on foreign children's books for new blood: Hergé, Thorbjorn Egner, Wilhelm Matthissen, Amund Schroder and Astrid Lindgren all appear in the spring 1959 list.

Those who worked there throughout the fifties remember conditions as 'old-fashioned'. By later standards the firm was

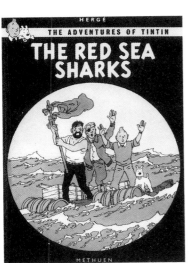

understaffed and in consequence everyone worked very hard. The prevailing atmosphere was kindly and courteous, with great attention paid to detail. In retrospect, salaries and money generally seem to ex-employees to have been rather stingy, but personal problems would always be listened to with sympathy and an attempt made to offer help. From the editor's point of view, Alan White's policy of basic non-interference was the right one and perhaps was part of the reason why people still tended to stay with the firm until they retired. Fifty years' service was quite frequent, as the board's minutes show in their records of long-service presentations. In many ways it's as if the spirit of Algernon Methuen was still hovering beneficently over the company, but what was true of Methuen was still true of the country as a whole. There was a *gravitas* about fifties Britain which the sixties would dispel, and in some senses Victorian Britain didn't end until over half-way through the twentieth century.

(*left*) Brendan Behan
(*right*) Bertolt Brecht

In Peter Wait (although not himself an academic) Methuen had, according to several contemporaries, one of the finest academic publishers of the time. He is remembered as ceaselessly trawling the universities for new authors. Two of those he attracted were Peter Medawar and Konrad Lorenz. Medawar's Reith Lectures of 1959 on *The Future of Man* were published in 1960. The psychology series was strong too, with Eysenck as one of the readers. Gradually Methuen was able through its

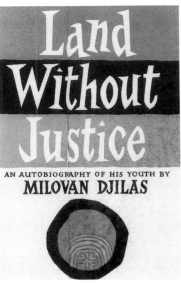

substantial list, especially on this side, to pull away from the early post-war problems and become a desirable bed-fellow for other publishers wanting economies of scale. The Methuen–Crosthwaite-Eyre negotiations rumbled on and were finalised in May 1957. Colonel Oliver Crosthwaite-Eyre was made deputy chairman of Methuen and a parent company was established in June 1958 as Associated Book Publishers. There was to be an amalgamation of sales and production departments but the three houses, Methuen, Chapman and Hall and Eyre and Spottiswoode, were to remain editorially distinct within the group.

The Methuen catalogue shows no immediate shift of emphasis following the merger, though ex-employees remember tensions between the parts of the new conglomerate arising quite quickly as a a struggle for dominance of the group began. 1958 saw the same interest in European literature: John Willett on *The Theatre of Bertolt Brecht*, Milovan Djilas's *Land Without Justice*, Antonia White's translation of Montgeurre's *Thou Shalt Love*, the Nobel prizewinner Halldor Laxness's *The Happy Warriors*, more Anouilh and Giraudoux and the first *Tintin*. British fiction is represented by John Coates's continuation of Jane Austen's fragment *The Watsons*, A. P. Herbert's *Made for Man* and Honor Tracy's *The Prospects Are Pleasing*; R. K. Narayan is the brightest representative of English Literature with *The Guide*. The Arden Shakespeare has three new titles and The Revels series is represented by *The Changeling*, while Cynewulf's *Elene* stands in for the Anglo-Saxon series. There is a new Venture Library, edited by Patrick Thornhill, of abridged classics for eleven- to sixteen-year-olds, of Buck and Bennett, and H. G. Wells. The lists of pure and applied science books read like the shape of things to come. For children there were *Atoms and Energy* and *Radioastronomy and Radar*, and for adults *Protein Structure* and *General Circuit Theory*. The lines had been laid down that would at last change the whole tone and pace of twentieth-century life.

# Methuen
# Books

autumn and winter
# 1963-4

# EIGHT

# *The Play's The Thing*
## 1960–81

History doesn't, of course, divide itself into significant decades, and it's therefore coincidental that the greatest change in Methuen, foreshadowing the most recent events in the firm's history, should coincide with the beginning of the sixties. It's possible to see, and I think without too much distortion, the real shift to a consumer-based society with all its implications for Britain and ultimately for publishing as well, inherent in Methuen's absorption into the Associated Book Publishers conglomerate.

Peter Medawar's 1954 Reith lectures, *The Future of Man*, which Methuen published in 1960, tidied up the first half of the twentieth century's knowledge about humankind, while 'the cream of APH' as the catalogue calls it, Herbert's *Look Back and Laugh*, set the closing seal on the 'man of letters', the all-rounder who was able to make a name and a living from the ceaseless production of literary ephemera from which the more solid books like *The Water Gipsies* and *Holy Deadlock* jutted out like rocks in a sea of froth. In future, writers were to be increasingly confined and defined as poet, novelist, dramatist, journalist and screenwriter, a trend that has only begun to reverse again in the 1980s as writers find it increasingly difficult to make a living, or even find a sufficient audience, in one medium alone.

Michael Turner, who was eventually to become chairman of ABP and who had joined Methuen as a reader in 1953 following Katharine Whitehorn's departure, remembers 'how wonderfully forthcoming A. P. Herbert was to someone junior' and his fund of often outrageous stories, sometimes told against himself. One of his favourites, which harked back to wartime on river patrol in *The Water Gipsies*, described how, when he found the Methuen building on fire and water from the firemen's hoses pouring into the basement where the stock was kept, Herbert was arrested for looting when, like a typical author, he began trying to rescue copies of his own books.

Methuen continued to expand its Modern Plays series, publishing the text almost as soon as they reached the stage. In 1960 the first play by a black woman writer to reach Broadway and subsequently London, Lorraine Hansberry's *a raisin in the sun*, was joined by John Arden's *Serjeant Musgrave's Dance*, and by Harold Pinter's *The Caretaker* and a trilogy of his earlier plays, *The Birthday Party*, *The Room* and *The Dumb Waiter*.

An interesting technological development was Methuen's excursion into talking books, which first appear in the catalogue in autumn 1960. 'The LP records, which are contained in a pocket inside the front cover of the books, are seven inches in diameter, of very high quality and unbreakable. The full-colour laminated covers are seven and a half inches square and the insets are lavishly illustrated and finely printed.' The titles included singing games and nursery rhymes, courses in dancing and keep fit, bird song and folk song, and John Betjeman reading *The Story of Jesus*. Julian Holland, reviewing them in the *Evening News*, called them 'the most important innovation in the world of the gramophone since the introduction of long-playing records'.

The catalogues show the publishing team as still J. Alan White as chairman, Peter Wait and John Cullen as joint managing directors by autumn 1961, the other directors being Anthony S. Forster (editorial), Frank Herrmann (production), Piers Raymond (sales), Patrick Thornhill (educational books) and Michael Turner (promotion). E. V. Rieu and Peter Wait were still editing the Methuen Modern Classics in the expanding educational list and there was, in autumn 1960, a new venture to cater for the 'university students, whose number is swelling rapidly both at home and overseas', and who 'are feeling the need of standard academic works in a cheaper form. Too often books they require for their studies cost twenty-five shillings or more.' To answer this need, the University Paperbacks Series was first published on 6 October 1960 in a clutch of thirteen at either twelve and six or seven and six, less than half the price of a hardback. The first titles included Einstein's *Relativity* and Eliot's *The Sacred Wood*, drawn from the Methuen backlist, but the intention was to include works from other publishers. The series was given its own symbol [**up**] (which I must confess I always believed stood for University Press, though which university I would have been at a loss to identify) and handsome glossy black-and-white and colour covers.

The series is remarkable as the first in the field of university paperbacks, showing that what some have categorised as Methuen's rather haphazard system of working with a great deal of editorial initiative and responsibility, was capable of divining a market and creating the product to fill it efficiently and elegantly. Originally conceived by Peter Wait and Tony Forster, the series was able in the sixties to print and sell out 10,000 copies a title. The series is also in a strange way the final justification of Algernon Methuen's own foresight, doing in its own time what he had tried to do in terms of the ill-fated Standard Library sixty years before. The books were to appear in larger batches at six-monthly intervals, a piece of daring

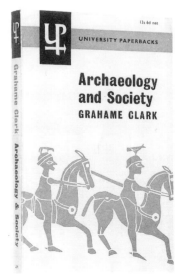

(*left*) Peter Wait

(*right*) John Cullen

which showed the devisers' understanding of the need to establish a strong image for the new series among the students who formed this rapidly expanding market.

In 1961 the Talking Books series was expanded to include language courses in French, German, Italian and Spanish. Again, this shows the firm's ability to respond quickly to social change. The new titles were aimed at the increasing numbers of British holiday-makers anxious to try out the two hundred most needed phrases reproduced on the record by 'expert native speakers'. The series was called Traveller Pocket Language Courses, and the thirty-two-page booklet of text could be torn from the record sleeve and carried away on holiday in the pocket.

The death of Una Ellis-Fermor and the edition of her last book, *Shakespeare The Dramatist*, put together as a tribute by Kenneth Muir in autumn 1961, also has an end-of-era implication. She had been responsible for the post-war revision of one of the pillars of the Methuen list, the Arden Shakespeare, which was now under the general editorship of Harold Brooks and Harold Jenkins, and it is fair to say that it was her combination of industry and critical acumen that had discerned the need to set the project on its way.

It isn't clear at which point precisely Sir H. Nutcombe Hume was replaced as chairman of the group by Colonel Oliver Crosthwaite-Eyre. The directors' minutes for Methuen end in

June 1959 just before the Annual General Meeting, with Sir Nutcombe Hume still in the chair, but the autumn list for 1958 gives Alan White as chairman. The 1959 and 1960 catalogues give no details of directors. By 1961, when details of the board appear again, Alan White is once more cited as chairman. By then radical changes had begun to be made. The new chairman had decided to broaden the original Associated Book Publishers group of three more or less autonomous houses, and as the very successful legal publishers Sweet and Maxwell were also looking for an amalgamation, because as a combined family firm they were susceptible to takeover, the group was expanded to include them.

There were both advantages and disadvantages in this new development. Methuen's financial affairs had continued to be organised under the accounting aegis of the company secretary Leonard Youthed, who had been with the firm since Sir Algernon's time. It is alleged by some employees that the new management were taken aback by the seeming haphazardness of the financial side, and the Sweet and Maxwell directors were given the job of tightening it all up. Nevertheless, from a practical point of view the methods had been successful in producing not only books but profit, and on the academic side, at least, Methuen had a bigger turnover than Sweet and Maxwell. However, times were changing and there was now to be a much greater emphasis on money. Tony Forster, who was to become managing director in 1969 and chairman when Peter Wait retired in 1973, remembers: 'Publishing became big business at that time. There was a lot of interest from American firms, a lot of takeovers. It became a growth industry, therefore the commercial considerations tended to become important.' Michael Turner also remembers the big development of promotional and marketing concepts and departments in the late fifties and early sixties throughout the publishing industry.

The change made little immediate difference to the appearance of the list. The drama section continued to grow impressively with more plays by Shelagh Delaney, John Arden and Harold Pinter and the addition of Henry Livings. From abroad there was more Bertolt Brecht, Max Frisch and Rolf Hochhuth. To the children's list had been added a number of non-fiction series: Methuen's Outlines, Story Biographies, the Young World series and the Children Everywhere series, while Tintin, the Bruna and Babar books, and Ruth Manning-Sanders's classic re-telling of fairy stories illustrated by Robin Jaques supplied the staple fiction.

The first real evidence of the changes taking place appears in the spring list of 1964. Though Alan White is still chairman, and Peter Wait and John Cullen are joint vice-chairmen, the managing director is John Burke from Sweet and Maxwell. But most important of all, the company has moved from the 36

Essex Street premises, where it had been for nearly seventy years, to Sweet and Maxwell's glass and concrete tower block at 11 New Fetter Lane. It is this move that accounts in part for the paucity of Methuen archive material. Peter Wait remembers during the last days at Essex Street, being ankle-deep in torn-up correspondence and records which must have included letters from writers like Conrad, Henry James, Kipling, Wells and Bennett, dating from the firm's very earliest times. Michael Turner rescued a batch of E. H. Shepard originals for *The Wind in the Willows* which had been thrown out into the corridor as rubbish. The Essex Street offices were a 'tatty friendly place' and much lamented. At the same time the new company was making plans to withdraw from Book Centre as a system of warehousing and distribution, and plans were made to build a new warehouse and office outside London in Andover. In this way the move signals a very real break with the past, to be reflected eventually in a radical re-division of the areas of publishing activity within the new group.

Tony Forster describes these changes in his memoir.

> The functions of the different firms are much more closely defined. Methuen Educational was founded simply to deal with school books, and then Methuen became the academic division. And the general division came to be called Eyre Methuen. I myself, and Peter Wait, lost all our scientific books which went to Chapman and Hall, who in their turn lost their general books and became an entirely scientific and technical company. And Methuen became purely publishers of university books and we hadn't the right to pick up a biography or something else. Art books went to the general division to John Cullen, so we lost those.

The Methuen imprint was run by Peter Wait as a university list largely devoted to the Humanities, with the new Arden Shakespeare as its core, until his retirement in 1973, when Tony Forster carried it on until 1978. The imprint which most clearly resembles the original Methuen was the general division, eventually renamed Eyre Methuen. However, these changes weren't finalised until 1971. Alan White retired in 1969 and John Cullen became chairman of Methuen, Eyre and Spottiswoode, an overlong title which was slimmed down to Eyre Methuen in 1972 with the amalgamation of the two general lists as 'a symbol simultaneously of the distinguished inheritance provided by Methuen and by Eyre and Spottiswoode and of their current working unity as the General Division of Associated Book Publishers'. Books were still being attributed in the catalogue to either Methuen or Eyre and Spottiswoode until 1972.

In spite of the move to New Fetter Lane in 1964, the Methuen

list for the next few years continued to look much as before until the disappearance of science, agriculture and mathematics in the autumn 1968 catalogue. The baby boom is reflected in an ever-expanding children's list, published from the mid-fifties onwards in a separate catalogue aimed at school libraries, which had been developing rapidly since the early fifties, especially in primary schools.

Methuen's most important native and resident fiction writer of the sixties was briefly John Berger, the Marxist art critic of the *New Statesman*, who began writing innovative novels with *A Painter of Our Time* published in 1958. His second novel, *The Foot of Clive*, was published by Methuen in 1962, after some acrimony over the jacket and illustrations. Berger's art background made it inevitable that he would take a more than usual interest in the physical appearance of his work at a time when it had become much less common for writers to be consulted on these matters. John Cullen wrote to Frank Herrmann in December 1961:

> I know that authors like John Berger with ideas for book jackets can be irritating but may I ask you – and perhaps some of the others in the production department who are not directly exposed to them – to be a little more accommodating in your attitude. Authors are after all the source of our activities. Their special relationship to their own work makes them sensitive to real or imagined slights, and a huffily disdainful manner is the easiest way to lose them. If Berger has an idea for a jacket he should surely not be regarded as a tiresome fellow who must be penalised for wasting time.

Perhaps when Frank Herrmann himself became an author, with a book for children called *The Giant Alexander*, he remembered the advice with pleasure.

Geoffrey Strachan, who was taken on by Cullen in 1961 as an editorial assistant, remembers him as kind and shy. During the sixties his health deteriorated, but in Leslie Lonsdale-Cooper (also, with Michael Turner, the co-translator of the Tintin books) he had an excellent senior editor who trained Strachan in the precise art of copy-editing. It's interesting to see how the twin skills of commissioning and editing are passed on in a firm, helping to perpetuate the tone of a particular imprint, and it's possible to see the training given by Cullen and Lonsdale-Cooper still manifesting itself nearly thirty years later. This makes for great continuity in a company, whatever external changes may take place by way of takeovers. What is really being bought and sold is a set of editors trained in a tradition and the consequent relationships between editors and authors which issue in the tangible form of a list. For this reason it is often difficult and always disruptive for a house to

11 New Fetter Lane

make any sudden change of direction, and certainly not while the senior management remains in place. The attempted changes in the style and direction of Methuen in the sixties had effectively to wait for the retirement of Alan White and John Cullen, though Tony Forster believed that these two were increasingly marginalised by the Sweet and Maxwell team of John Burke, Peter Allsop and Dennis Alcock.

It was *The Foot of Clive*, John Berger's first novel for Methuen, that Geoffrey Strachan was given by John Cullen as a test to read and report on when he applied for a job with the company in 1961, and it became his first recommendation. He was soon dividing the reading pile with Leslie Lonsdale-Cooper and was then made responsible for drama and humour, which were to be his chief concerns until October 1973, when John Cullen indicated that since his own retirement was approaching Strachan would have to assume a much wider general responsibility for what was now the combined general list of Eyre Methuen, a name it would keep until 1982, when it would revert to Methuen.

The early attempt to give the whole group more direction and corporateness is reflected in the training course which took place in 1964 and 1965 and for which some of the papers still survive. Tony Forster, who delivered a talk on academic publishing, remembers the atmosphere as 'bullish and optimistic'. He particularly mentions the appearance of the 'egg-head paperback' as the most interesting recent development and particularly the Methuen University Paperbacks series, which by January 1965 numbered over a hundred titles. Forster travelled abroad – he was the first member of the firm to go to Africa in 1965 in search of markets – and understood that:

> the increase in university education throughout the world – and not least in the poor and underdeveloped countries – has led to a big demand for cheaper academic books. A situation is rapidly being reached where professors and students are expecting standard books to be issued as paperbacks. . . . Our authors have had to accept a lower royalty on their books in paperback, but the increase in sales have much increased their income (and ours!).

Forster himself had been responsible for the Little Library of Art, which were originally French publications handsomely illustrated but cheap enough for the average or student pocket.

Peter Wait's paper on scientific publishing makes the Methuen contribution quite distinct within the group as he saw it:

> Roughly speaking Methuen is the only firm in the group with much biology, geology and statistics. Typically

The Little Library of Art stand

Chapman and Hall, when they do do books on biology etc., do them for agriculturalists; ours are for universities.... Chapman and Hall, and Spon, tend to look for their books among the technologists, while Methuen look for theirs among the pure scientists.

It's clear that Methuen, the publishers of three Nobel prize-winners, Tinbergen, Von Frisch and Lorenz (whose *King Solomn's Ring*, published in 1952, was a worldwide bestseller), regarded themselves as the academic élite of the group. Eventually, however, they were to lose their cherished scientific side to Chapman and Hall in further divisionalisation.

Wait's comments on his methods are revealing too.

The only way to get books out of first-class people is to ask them. They never offer to write, and do not often willingly agree. Ideally therefore one should spend most

of one's time meeting people, finding out what books need writing, who ought to write them, and then asking these people. Without a large perambulatory editorial staff this is not possible. It is to remedy this situation that one has recourse to outside editors. For the monographs we have altogether five. They are paid a fee for every title published. Every now and then they write in and say that so-and-so would like to do a book on such-and-such, and that this is a good idea; sometimes they say why don't I write to so-and-so and ask him to write; sometimes I write to them and say 'X' has a fascinating article in the *New Scientist* and why don't we ask the writer to do a book on it.

It was a method Wait had developed along with E. V. Rieu at first for schools and then for university books, and once again it illustrates the importance and tenacity of tradition in the firm. Unfortunately, John Cullen's contribution to the training course, which Peter Wait refers to in his paper, hasn't survived for an insight into his views on general publishing. Wait notes in a parenthesis to be expanded during his talk that by the mid-sixties the home trade in general books, including fiction, was static 'with almost no increase in the last few years.... The biggest chance of expanding our profits lies in the field of scholarly and educational books.' Wait also noted that since the Second World War English had ousted German as the language of science.

The general decline in the profitability of hard-cover fiction which Peter Wait describes was to continue throughout the sixties until in 1969 Booker and subsequently other prizes began the long process of refocusing public attention on fiction. This decline, which was to reach its nadir in some publishers' contention that the novel was dead, had a variety of causes which Geoffrey Strachan analyses as both organisational and cultural. He sees, in particular, a lack of sufficient paperback outlets for literary fiction. This meant that young readers were unable to afford copies of contemporary novels by new writers to buy, read and become intimate with as they could with the plays published by Methuen, which were virtually all published in paperback. The Methuen Modern Plays series published new drama in simultaneous hard and paper cover soon after it was staged and the Playscripts series, started in 1965, published plays by new writers in paperback only, very cheaply and quickly produced.

In terms of format and price these paperback editions, like the University Paperbacks and other publishers' similar series were what the Americans and later the British were to call 'trade paperbacks' as opposed to 'mass market paperbacks' (i.e. they were designed to be sold in bookshops – via the book trade – not at railway station bookstalls). Trade paperbacks

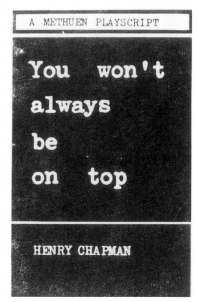

tended to be the same page size as hard cover books and often printed on the same quality paper. The price might be about half the price of a hardback. Thus in the mid sixties when hardcover editions of plays were priced at about fifteen shillings, paperback Modern Plays and Playscripts were priced at about seven and sixpence.

Briefly in the mid sixties Methuen tried simultaneously hard and paper cover publication for fiction, beginning with Jakov Lind's *Landscape in Concrete* published alongside three other novels in paperback, but the experiment failed, among other reasons because bookshops simply had nowhere to display this new animal – a large format twelve and sixpenny trade paperback novel – at a time when paperback novels were generally published in Penguin-style format at prices around three to five shillings, based on minimum print runs of fifteen or twenty thousand copies. Methuen sold fewer copies of the paperback edition of *Landscape in Concrete* than they did of the hard cover. So fleeting was this exercise that it didn't even make its way into the catalogue. It was an experiment before its time, when foreign fiction in translation was increasingly difficult to sell, and with a somewhat austere design more appropriate to the University Paperbacks series.

It's hard to believe, though, that the collapse of fiction publishing was merely the result of an insufficiently developed supply of cheap books. Had there been a great enough demand some means would surely have been found to satisfy it. The explanation has to be cultural as well as technical. One important aspect was that drama was now seen as a serious art form to be included for study in university syllabuses. It was still a period of great excitement in the theatre, fuelled by a policy of public subsidy which allowed the development not only of large national companies but also of provincial theatres like the Belgrade, Coventry, and the Nottingham Playhouse and in the second or, from some points of view, third wave, encouraged the rise of 'fringe' theatre and Theatre-in-Education. Methuen supported each of these waves in turn, not only with the publication of plays but also by taking part in conferences which led to public debate that kept the pot boiling (in particular organising an event with the Nottingham Playhouse on regional theatre), and in the early seventies by initiating and supporting for three years the launch of the magazine *Theatre Quarterly*.

In contrast, contemporary fiction was still largely an optional course in English departments of universities, where it was still common to begin with *Beowulf* and finish with Hardy, and the emphasis was on the study of past texts rather than, as with the new drama departments, on an appraisal of current forms and developments.

Excitement was further engendered by the campaign to free the theatre from the censoring attentions of the Lord

Chamberlain's office. In 1966 Methuen published as a Play-script at six shillings Edward Bond's *Saved*, which had been refused a licence for public performance and had had to be performed at the Royal Court Theatre, which, as the English Stage Society, was able to make the public members of a very exclusive club. The impact of the play is perhaps hard now to reconstruct. Penelope Gilliat wrote in the *Observer*: 'The play is about English thuggishness; it is our Fascist document, the one we don't want to know about.' A quarter of a century later the social problem that *Saved* presents still hasn't been resolved.

*Early Morning*, Bond's next play in 1968, which was the last play to be banned in its entirety by the Lord Chamberlain's office before George Strauss's Bill to abolish theatre censorship became law in September 1968, threw up grave problems with publication, outlined by Geoffrey Strachan in an internal memo to John Cullen on 10 April. Methuen took legal advice, and on counsel's opinion that only the name Lady Flora Hastings and the legend prefacing the work, 'The events of this play are true', might be likely to provoke prosecution for either civil or criminal libel, offered to publish *Early Morning* at the end of May. Sadly for Methuen, Bond, anxious at the delay, had agreed by then to let John Calder publish it, though he returned to the Methuen list with his subsequent work.

Bond, however, didn't provide the only theatrical *cause célèbre*. In early 1967 Methuen published Joe Orton's *Loot* and made arrangements to follow this with the double bill *Crimes of Passion*, which the Royal Court was to stage in June. Orton came back from a holiday in North Africa for the first night and Geoffrey Strachan remembers talking to him on the theatre steps. Two months later Orton was dead, brutally murdered by his lover Kenneth Halliwell, and the book's title had become appallingly prophetic.

Not all the drama list was as immediately arresting, but what seemed an endless series of interesting productions and subsequent publications was backed up by the critical writing and editing of John Russell Taylor (*Anger and After*, *The New Wave*), Charles Marowitz and Simon Trussler (*The Encore Reader*, *Theatre at Work*). Theatre catered for a student population that wanted the trappings of a night out at a price it could afford, and for opportunities for intellectual excitement and discussion. Looking at the lists, however, it is remarkable how male-dominated, with the exceptions of Joan Littlewood and Ann Jellicoe, the theatre and therefore Methuen's drama output at this time remains. For women writers, novels were still the most accessible route to a mass audience and one in which it was possible once more by the mid-sixties to produce work the equivalent, in terms of the further exploration of modernist structures, of what was being done in the theatre.

Nevertheless, publishers experienced hardback literary fiction as increasingly difficult to sell. Writers were urged to

Christopher Isherwood, drawn
by Don Bachardy

abandon it for non-fiction – biography, criticism, social and cultural history – for which there was still a market in the institutional buying of libraries of every kind. Advertising and review space were increasingly devoted to non-fiction and the institutional market. The market for fiction became more and more the public libraries with their need for genre titles, many of which would subsequently find their way into mass paperbacks. Many bookshops ceased to stock hardback fiction at all, apart from the occasional bestseller.

Methuen's new fiction titles in 1967, when they were publishing Joe Orton, John Arden, John Mortimer, David Cregan and Heinar Kipphardt on their drama list, were Pearl Buck, A. P. Herbert, Honor Tracy, Howard Fast and Jakov Lind. 'Already by the mid-sixties,' Geoffrey Strachan remembers, 'John Cullen was feeling defeated. It had become very difficult to continue to publish foreign novelists in translation as he had done, even people like Michel Butor and Max Frisch, with whose plays we did well.... Was there a retreat from fiction by young readers? Was it viewed as an élitist form? Was there a retreat from print culture generally in the second half of the sixties?'

He records a similar retreat from writers' theatre round about the same time, towards directors and their improvisational group theatre. With the increasing dominance of television, verbal culture was everywhere under pressure. Non-fiction books, if they were to compete, had to be lavishly and photographically illustrated.

Yet among the books which Geoffrey Strachan sees as Methuen's most important post-war publications, and alongside the plays by Bond and Orton in particular, he points to a novel and a book of verse: Isherwood's *A Single Man* (1964) and Brecht's *Poems 1913–1956*. Methuen eventually became Isherwood's sole publishers in paperback after Penguin had begun to relinquish their rights in his books in the mid-seventies and Methuen finally started their own fiction trade paperback series in the early eighties: Methuen Modern Fiction. *A Single Man* continues Methuen's long tradition of publishing the work of homosexual writers which had begun with Wilde's *De Profundis*. It was always Isherwood's favourite among his novels, and it's indicative of the trough into which publishing, and the publishing of fiction in particular, had fallen, that Penguin were willing to let such an important twentieth-century figure go out of print in the seventies.

Towards the end of the sixties and in the early seventies new fiction names do begin to appear in the amalgamated list: J. P. Donleavy, John Braine, Bernice Rubens, Chaim Bermant, Bernard Malamud, but these are all from the Eyre and Spottiswoode stable. Methuen contributions come notably from David Nobbs and Barry Cole. However, from the appearance of the second amalgamated catalogue in June 1969 drama, as

Bertolt
Brecht

Poems
1913-1956
Eyre Methuen

Methuen's unique contribution, is given an eye-catching coloured section of its own.

The publication of Brecht's *Poems* in 1976, edited by John Willett, was John Cullen's swansong, produced after his retirement from full-time work at Methuen in 1974, the year which brought the beginning of a fortunately temporary crisis in Methuen's finances and in publishing generally. The Associated Book Publishers accountants warned that there would have to be cut-backs in publishing in 1975 and the first round of staff redundancies came in autumn 1974, a few months after Geoffrey Strachan had taken over as managing director and while John Cullen was still the chairman, coming in two or three days a week.

Those of us who were publishing or being published at the time remember the collective hysteria, the panic that seemed to have gripped the entire book trade as we pursued the rumours of collapse on every side, of staff made redundant and entire lists suspended. The reasons were many and complex, but some have become clearer with time. National inflation and the oil crisis, which not only increased the price of books themselves but ensured that there was less money in the public's purse to spend on them anyway, was of course a hugely contributing factor, but it would be a dangerously complacent mistake to think that the industry itself had contributed nothing to its own downfall and that there are no lessons to be learned, chief among them that of too great a reliance on the institutional market, with the subsequent neglect of merchandising and a failure to sell to the general public. A whiff of gentlemanliness and a barely disguised contempt for the public, the bookseller and the author still characterised too many publishers. In this respect John Cullen's letter on John Berger's right to make suggestions about his jacket is refreshingly unusual. Michael Turner also emphasises the respect for authors of the ABP top management Dennis Alcock and Peter Allsop.

Perhaps the most important aspect of the crisis is the publishers' collective acquiescence in the difficulty of finding an audience for fiction, to the point where they were prepared in company with booksellers to write off the novel as an obsolete art form, a deduction which the eighties has fortunately shown to be untrue. Even the supposedly impossible-to-market short story is enjoying a renaissance. Because art isn't progressive in the sense in which scientists and information technologists may use the term, an art form is always capable of resuscitation, of re-invention. With literature it is the function of all those engaged in its making and promotion to be constantly watchful and innovatory in enabling it to be produced and find its public. Publishing houses need to be more, not less, than well-run businesses (as the imaginative promotion of the Methuen drama list shows) unless they are content to be merely suppliers

of necessary data-packs. A neglect of literature ultimately brings books themselves into disregard.

A niggardly public subsidy from the Arts Council in the seventies, parallel to the much greater public investment in theatre, helped to keep contemporary British fiction alive, while ways were being found in the industry to promote it adequately by a combination of increased paperback outlets and publicity mainly provided by the new fiction prizes. Whatever may be thought of the disadvantages of a prize system, prizes do give books an aura of excitement which is necessary to any art form, mixed as they all are with commerce, fashion and the entertainment industry. However, British literature is too important to be left exclusively to the private sector, and some degree of public intervention is needed whether by the prince, the church, the state or the multinational corporation.

In 1976 Methuen, realising that the answer to the financial crisis must ultimately lie in increased sales, began its own mass paperback imprint, first called simply Methuen Paperbacks and then, in 1977, Magnum. For a time this looked as if it might be a success: turnover was high and there was a small boom in sales, which faded out at the beginning of the eighties into a sizeable loss. Ironically, Methuen's two paperback bestsellers of the seventies were versions of the trade paperback from the humour list. Originally published in 1971 and lavishly illustrated, *Monty Python's Big Red Book* sold 70,000 copies before going into trade paperback in 1972 to sell a further 140,000 in its first year, and has since sold another 400,000 copies. The book had of course had a flying start as a film and television spin-off, but new material was created, principally by Eric Idle for the printed version, and even more for the sequel in 1973, *The Brand New Monty Python Bok*, which sold twice as many copies in first hard cover and then paperback, and has now sold over three-quarters of a million. Robert Hewison has described the Python phenomenon in his own book for Methuen, *Monty Python: The Case Against*, published in 1981. Speaking of the impact of the first television series, he writes, '*Monty Python* quickly became a cult. . . . Its energy and enthusiasm transmitted itself to the audience, who rejoiced in the absurdity of it all.' Throughout the publishing history of the Python books, Methuen and in particular, Geoffrey Strachan, as editor and managing director, had to walk a tight rope between self-censorship and possible prosecution for obscenity, blasphemy and criminal libel. The most tricky of all was *The Life of Brian*, published in 1979 just after the trial and successful conviction for blasphemy of *Gay News*'s editor for publishing a poem about Christ by James Kirkup with homosexual implications.

The other bestselling series for adults in trade paperback was the Thelwell books, which had begun to appear as paperbacks in the early seventies. These were followed by the most popular children's books, but in a standard paperback size – a field in

New books
January-July 1976
including Methuen
Paperbacks

Irreverence,
scurrility,
profanity,
vilification and
licentious abuse:
MONTY PYTHON
THE CASE AGAINST

Robert Hewison

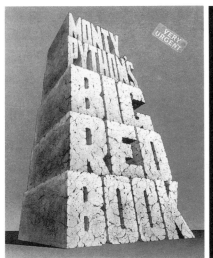

1971

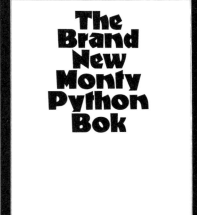

1973

1977

1979

1983

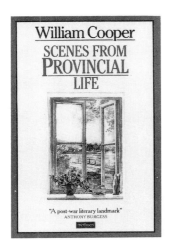

which Penguin's Puffins were the only other contenders. When the rest of the adult paperback list was subsumed into Methuen's general list again in the eighties the children's books, continued both in hard and soft cover while the adult trade paperbacks based on the success of the drama and humour titles were joined by quality fiction.

Those who worked for Methuen in the sixties and seventies in the editorial and promotional side remember it in spite of the cyclical financial crises as a good time of great friendliness among the staff and dedication to publishing quality work. The foray in the late seventies into the mass paperback market made them less happy both because of the uncertainties of this new field and the general lack of expertise in it, and because they were in a sense abandoning quality for quantity. However, this wasn't new in the company's history. Algernon Methuen himself had published a great deal which he thought of doubtful literary value in order to go on publishing the work he believed in, like early Henry James and Joseph Conrad and T. S. Eliot's *The Sacred Wood*. Michael Turner recalls that increasingly, however, what had been implicit in earlier Methuen practice that the most important part of a publishing house was its authors, had to be stated as a conscious principle against the demands of the parent company's financial managers.

# *And so on . . .*

Gradually the firm and publishing generally recovered from the shocks of the early and mid-seventies, and although it became clear that the mass paperback enterprise was a financial failure, good house management enabled the company to publish its way out of any difficulty that might have followed. New blood was brought in from Weidenfeld in the persons of Christopher Falkus, as chairman of Eyre Methuen, and Alan Miles, who as managing director of ABP (UK) introduced a new system of individually pricing titles on their market expectations, rather than the mark-up formula based on the unit production cost and royalty rate which had been in operation for the previous twenty years.

By 1981 the Eyre and Spottiswoode part of the general list had dwindled to a rump and it no longer seemed to make sense to continue with the Eyre Methuen imprint. Methuen, now known as Methuen London, became once more the general list from the time of the spring 1982 catalogue. At the same time there was an attempt by the parent company to strengthen the relationship between it and its publishing arms. This made an excellent structure to carry publishing forward into the eighties, and the increasingly full and glossy catalogues reflect this.

It is too early to make judgements on the individual writers who appear in them but, in particular, the children's and drama lists show growth and exuberance. Children's books especially cover the full range of price and age group from books for babies to teenage novels in their own special insert. A glance at, for example, the catalogue for spring 1986 shows Methuen responding to the impact of feminism with new titles by and about women, recalling the interests in the New Woman at the beginning of the century; H. V. Morton's *In Search of Wales* for the first time in paperback; Babar, Pooh, and *The Wind in The Willows* and Dick Bruna's people still in business; Thelwell and Monty Python supporting the humour; the drama list republishing Methuen's first playwright Ibsen along with Brecht, Orton, Anouilh and Pinter, a backlist against which new writers can find their own voice.

Yet the very success of publishing in the eighties and the communications explosion has made the industry vulnerable

to the destabilising phenomenon of takeover. When Methuen became a public company in the 1920s it must have seemed that the shares given to workers would perhaps help to keep wolves at bay, and indeed the Crosthwaite-Eyre family stake in the company, which became the strongest element in the late fifties, was relied on to do the same thing. But public companies are inevitably subject to change in shareholding and the Crosthwaite-Eyre family interest was gradually reduced to 35 per cent. The Associated Book Publishers Board had tried to guard their backs by making contingency plans with a merchant bank. At the crucial moment this strategy proved insufficient and Methuen found themselves, in 1987, sold with the rest of ABP to International Thomson, who then sold the Methuen general and children's lists on to Paul Hamlyn's Octopus Publishing Group, itself a member of the Reed International Group. This occasioned a further move in April 1988 from New Fetter Lane to Michelin House in the Fulham Road.

Methuen's experience exemplifies the problems of established publishing houses in the eighties, which so often are a reflection of those of society at large: how to maintain an identity, a quality, in an age of corporation and mass consumerism where more may not necessarily mean better, and the individual book and its creator must find a profitable slot in the market place if it is to reach an audience and convey its unique voice to the reader; how indeed to publish effectively both Corelli and Conrad. After a hundred years the parameters have inevitably changed, but the central question faced by Algernon Stedman when he went into business in 1889 to create Messrs Methuen remains the same.

# Index